Also by Stuart N. Hampshire

Spinoza

Freedom of the Individual

Thought & Action

Age of Reason:
The Seventeenth-Century Philosophers
(editor)

Philosophy of Mind
(editor)

Modern Writers and Other Essays

MODERN
WRITERS
AND OTHER
ESSAYS

Stuart N. Hampshire

Alfred A. Knopf New York 1970

ABIGAIL E. WEEKS MEMORIAL LIBRARY
UNION COLLEGE
BARBOURVILLE, KENTUCKY

809
H231

This is a Borzoi Book
Published by Alfred A. Knopf, Inc.

Copyright © 1960, 1961, 1962, 1963, 1965, 1966, 1967, 1968, 1969 by Stuart N. Hampshire.
All rights reserved under International and Pan-American Copyright Conventions.
Published in the United States by Alfred A. Knopf, Inc., New York.
Originally published in Great Britain by Chatto & Windus Ltd.
Library of Congress Catalog Card Number: 79–88746
Manufactured in the United States of America

First American Edition

Preface

All the essays in this book originally appeared as articles or reviews in various periodicals. I have made some changes. I thank the editors of the following periodicals for their cooperation and permissions:

New Statesman: "Letters of James Joyce," "Sade," "Letters of Oscar Wilde," "Henry James," "Wittgenstein," "Proust II," "Edmund Burke," "George Eliot's Essays," "Modern Tragedy," "A Ruinous Conflict."

The New York Review of Books: Introduction, "W. H. Auden," "Virginia Woolf," "E. M. Forster," "The Theatre of Sade," "Freud and Lou Andreas-Salomé," "William James," "The Autobiography of Bertrand Russell I," "The Autobiography of Bertrand Russell II."

Encounter: "Proust I," "Pasternak's *Doctor Zhivago*."

The Listener: "Letters of Freud."

Score: "A Composer's World."

Contents

CONTENTS

Introduction

THIS introduction is an apology. I am by training a philosopher, and not a critic. I need to explain how I came to write these essays over a period of about twenty years, and why I put them together now. There is, I believe, a connecting interest, and a unity of approach, in the book; and this interest connects work in philosophy with a more scattered reviewing of literature.

There are a set of needs, sometimes amounting to obsessions, which only philosophical argument can satisfy. Some of these obsessions are found, as incitements to the imagination, in writers who are superficially quite unlike each other, and who never themselves entered into philosophical argument. Many of the high abstractions of philosophy, theories of reality and illusion and theories of the self, have their more concrete equivalents, an apt expression, or even a kind of translation, in a personal style of fiction, or of rhetoric, or of poetry. When one works back to the philosophical ideas that are suggested by idiosyncrasies of form and method in fiction, the translation sometimes helps to explain the hold that a novelist or poet has had upon one, when other explanations fall short. There is a middle ground of inner conflict and uncertainty, which may be expressed, and also resolved, in argument, and which may also be expressed and resolved indirectly, in some imaginative experiment with language.

Approaching the middle ground from the other side,

one may see some of the abstract arguments, which are the substance of philosophy, as permanently interesting, partly because they reveal the imaginative needs of a temperament of a recurring type, or because they are an indirect form of self-exploration, and of a typical rebelliousness; and this view may be justifiable, in spite of the rigour and generality which the philosopher could properly claim for his arguments and which alone can earn assent. Then one is impelled to turn to those writers who have not disguised their will to order the world in accordance with their imaginative needs: to novelists, poets, and moralists.

It is characteristic of modern philosophy that it is founded upon a distrust of philosophy. Some philosophers have seen philosophy as imperfectly satisfying intellectual needs which logic and mathematics will finally meet more adequately. Others have suspected that in philosophy, and particularly in moral philosophy and in the philosophy of psychology, strict argument is interesting only if it is also a working out of an imaginative vision. Some of those who belong to the second group, as I do, may have turned to philosophy in the first place, partly because of an early obsession with the power of the inherited vocabulary to set limits on their experience, and to veil and muffle their perceptions and their feelings. Perhaps they had felt themselves to be trapped within the normal resources of description, and had looked to the fiction and poetry of others for an escape from literalness. They will become philosophers or critics, if it is also for them a necessity that the liberation should come from the outside, and should have the impersonal authority either of argument or of scholarship.

So we become, for a time, Don Quixotes, enthralled by literary legends, accepting a picture of our own ambitions from favourite authors, because they had seemed the enemies of a deadening normality in the description of states of mind. Then the only way of establishing our own point of view is to travel from one original point of view to another. The solution is to analyse the power of the many different legends to which one still responds; critical comparisons become a necessity, if one is to be free to start again.

Among those who have expected most from the study of philosophy and from literature, there must be many who, like the present author, have thought of the common sense of ordinary speech as, among other things, a mechanism of defence, as often an instrument for disguising one's perceptions, and for simplifying thoughts and for taming the natural movements of self-assertion within the mind. In fact we know of this restlessness from countless testimonies, from *La Vie de Henri Brulard* to *Les Mots*. Common sense, and ordinary language, are not the least of the confinements in which one is brought up, swaddled, in the too long dependence upon ancestors, which is said to be both the disease and the distinction of the species. Customary categories and classifications were made long ago by others, and are part of a family inheritance. Although they can never be forgotten, they may still be resented, as any inheritance naturally may be, for being accidental and unchosen, for being contingent upon the date and circumstances of one's birth. For some temperaments this contingency of birth is very hard to accept at precisely the point where it sets limits on the true authorship of one's own thoughts. Therefore at a certain stage one is impelled to leave the linguistic home, and to look for the strange clothing that will fit a deviant and un-socialized consciousness. This is the stage at which one is overwhelmed by the aggressive eccentricity of some literary or philosophical imaginations which have constructed contrasting worlds: for example, by a metaphysician, such as Spinoza, or by the anti-metaphysicians, the logical positivists, who denied significance to many of the commonplace thoughts which one had been taught to echo: or by such novelists as Stendhal and Proust, who were inspired by the same desire for a recapture of selfishness, and for revenge upon the long prepared good sense of society. Only categories and classifications that seem wilfully disruptive and unsettling will seem to open the way to authenticity. The impulse is to peel customary words off experience, in the hope of confronting it again, without regard to the truths that are fittingly contained in socially approved forms of words. For social approval seems evidence of some convenient repression of disorderly thoughts and of the discarded experiences that they reflect.

Almost all the philosophers who have survived and are still read were to some degree subversive and unsettling, loosening the hold of accepted categories and habits of classification, and suggesting a scheme of description of their own design. This radical resistance to the usual certainties, and particularly to the usual pictures of the mind, is the beginning of philosphy, even if many philosophers have finally made peace with common sense, only on their own terms.

There is a familiar portrait of the mature philosopher as having passed through three stages: first, the innocent stage of acquiescence in the ordinary distinctions between reasonableness and unreasonableness: the second phase is one of aggressive scepticism, in which most accepted claims to knowledge, and to clear categorizations, seem quite unfounded; this may be represented as an adolescent phase of thought. Thirdly, there is a return, in maturity, to a disillusioned acceptance of the original commonplace categories, with the recognition that, with all their limitations, they are for us natural, and that it is only an adolescent dream that they might be made perfectly clear and transparent. Both Hume and Wittgenstein present this picture of a proper philosophical progress toward enlightenment; and it has convinced many, perhaps most, of my philosophical contemporaries. It represents mature philosophy as a kind of extended irony at the expense of intellectual enthusiasm, and at the expense of ambitious reconstructions of reality, which are neither strictly scientific nor in harmony with customary speech.

Certainly this story does represent many people's experience in philosophy, and particularly the experience of those who originally turned to philosophy because they were interested above all things in clarity of thought. For them the main service of philosophy is to ensure that they have, in ordinary language, clean instruments of thought, and that they need never commit themselves, either in speech or in writing, to more than they intend. They want to be protected against the risk of talking, and of thinking, insignificantly and with a doubtful purpose, and to be in full and self-conscious control of their words. They are always aware of the precariousness of sanity, and of the danger of uncontrolled speculation as a disease of the mind, often leading to monstrous growths of illusion. Perhaps they remember, as Hume and Wittgenstein could, abysses of doubt, morbid moments in their own thinking, against which a therapy is needed. A continual analysis of the structure of literal common-sense beliefs is for them a defence against those moments of dizziness, in which none of the normal connections of thought seemed secure. They will generally wish to reinforce the clear line that already divides the works of an irresponsible and literary imagination from the work of analytical philosophy, and to keep them even more definitely apart in separate compartments. Unintended, or not fully intended, meanings, and ambiguities of sense, can be the strength of imaginative writing, and they are to have no place in philosophy.

My own early, and present, concern with philosophy had a different, and, from one point of view, an opposite origin. I have looked in philosophy, as also in fiction and in poetry, not for a greater clarity in familiar ways of thought, but rather for a particular kind of confusion. The confusion is that which comes from trying conflicting possibilities of description, and from postponing a decision between them. It is the kind of confusion that occurs when one listens to different voices speaking different languages at the same time, and when one will not stop one's ears against all the voices other than the most familiar ones.

These very different demands made upon philosophy, and upon imaginative literature, must have an explanation in individual psychology. I do not claim that those who look in philosophy, as I do, for an escape from security, and for a certain kind of confusion, are right, and that those who value clarity and protection against illusion before all things are wrong. There are two psychological types, with different histories and emotional needs, who may perhaps complement each other.

Most of the essays and reviews reprinted here are attempts to indicate the points of divergence, or the controlling distortions, that mark an individual style, and that at the same time suggest a theory, or the sketch of a theory, of the natural movements of the mind and of their proper expression; and my assumption has been that the points of divergence are to be found in some history of inner conflict indirectly expressed. That is why several of these essays are concerned with letters and with biographical evidences.

Even apart from the brevity of the essays, and my own shortcomings, I could not pretend that any of the pieces amount to responsible literary criticism, which must surely be a balanced inquiry into the permanent substance of specific works. Rather they are short explorations from a rather eccentric starting-point, since the governing interest is first philosophical, and then psychological. I have looked for the origin of a peculiar use of a literary form, which can be interpreted as expressing philosophical ideas, and I have expected to find the origin of the ideas in the history of a temperament. My hypothesis has been that the sources, usually unconscious, of a personal style are often also the sources of a philosophical assumption, of a wilful redrawing of the distinction between appearances and reality, with the implied claim that one is thereby brought closer to a just description of experience. This hypothesis, which sonnects an individual style, a philosophical assumption and a psychological need, is far from being original. It can be found in Proust's *Contre Sainte-Beuve*, adn it is both a theme and a principle of construction in his novel. It can be found in other writers who cross, and re-cross, the line that is supposed to divide the kind of literary imagination, which is turned towards self-exploration and moral discovery, from philosophical ideas, which are necessarily abstract and general: in such dissimilar sources as Pater's *Plato and Platonism*, with its extraordinary penetration into the psychology of philosophy, in Buchner's *Wozzeck* and *Danton's Death*, in Ibsen, in parts of Freud, and of course the list could easily be extended. I hope that every writer considered in this volume to some degree illustrates the suggested connection, or is at least usefully considered from this point of view.

Among the philosophers, James, Russell, and Wittgenstein are also dramatic writers, makers of epigrams, and each was aware of the emotional needs which their own philosophies, and philosophy itself, must satisfy. They did not conceal either the temperamental or the imaginative sources of their own philosophical interests. James and Wittgenstein were nervous, hypochondriacal writers, confessional and egoistic, and their literary ambitions were not confined within the limits of philosophy, in the strict academic sense.

On the other side of the usual line, George Eliot, Proust, Joyce, Virginia Woolf, and E. M. Forster, each developed a complex and general thesis about their art, and about the necessity of fiction; and their principles of construction had a point of contact with metaphysical theories. They were at ease with abstractions, with theories of the self, and with theories of reality and illusion, and they tried to achieve in their writing a conversion, an awakening of self-awareness, which would shift attention from what they took to be the trivialities of experience to its original substance. They still command attention, partly because in their novels they disturb, and re-arrange, our usual picture of naturalness and artificiality in human behaviour.

The opposition between nature and artificiality, or convention, runs all through these essays, on these and other writers, as one unifying theme. Every person or theory considered here is concerned with some vision of the bedrock of human nature below its trivial and variable accretions. It is altogether obvious that political thought has always turned around this distinction, no less in Sartre than in Burke, and it is implicit in any serious theory of fiction. It is a distinction that seems to be indispensable, and yet it cannot be made precise. At least it is part of men's nature to have opinions about what their true nature is; but these opinions are in recurring conflict with each other. For example, those who accept Hume's and Burke's distinction between that which is natural and that which is artificial in men will count the observance of precedent and tradition as natural, and will count any philosophical questioning of them as artificial. Those, like Sade, who define man's nature in terms of his physical constitution will count moral traditions and social custom as artificial, and may mark the erotic and aggressive drives as constituting men's true nature. For a materialist the questioning of moral traditions is the beginning of a return to nature.

For these reasons the demand that men should find their way to a natural form of life is by itself an indeterminate demand. We can only imagine, and we do not know, what it would be like to find that way. No scientific inquiry will settle the dispute, because, from a scientific point of view, every human interest, and every feature of human behaviour, is equally a natural phenomenon to be explained. Human nature is so far not a scientific term, because it refers to what might exist, under ideal conditions which are not independently specified. Therefore the distinction seems irreducibly vague, a necessary prop of the moral imagination, and each conscious or unconscious moralist lends it a characteristic content. Henry James found a density of social relations, and an aesthetic sense of the past and of manners, the necessary expression and the necessary setting for the normal and natural life of men, without which they wither and are deprived of natural human feelings; as they were, according to James, in provincial America. For him naturalness was not innocence, but a fullness of experience; for him elaborated manners, which are a corruption of impulse, and a dramatic contrivance, save us from a dull and inhuman unconsciousness. His brother, William James, looked for a naturalness of an altogether different, almost an opposing, kind.

The force of the imagination in a personal style can make these various, and often contradictory, pictures of the natural condition of men plausible to us, provided only that they correspond to some sense of loss and of constraint which the reader still has. He may need this continuing conflict and variety, because they both protect and represent the confusion that is necessary to him, as being his natural state.

I

◄▮►

W. H. Auden

IT has sometimes been claimed that for several hundred years without interruption there has always been a major poet writing in the English language. Perhaps there have been some dull decades, for which the word 'major' would need to be stretched a little, when the already established resources of the language were just being steadily mined, without any new discoveries being made. Mr. Auden began to publish in a decade that was very far from being poetically dull. He was almost immediately recognized as likely to prolong the necessary line into the future. We have now arrived at the future, Mr. Auden is still writing, and the continuity holds.

The mature poetry of Eliot and Yeats surrounded Mr. Auden's beginnings, nearly forty years ago, when the first bright-jacketed Faber volumes began to appear. He was an intruder with a harsh voice, and, in *The Orators* and elsewhere, dramatized himself as an enemy of established poetical good manners. In his Preface to the *Oxford Book of Modern Verse*, Yeats showed his distaste for Auden's new reductive style, like a metaphysician of that time deploring the logical positivists. There was a respectful, veiled hostility between the generations. In the Thirties every English undergraduate who cared at all for contemporary writing kept these early Auden volumes with him, because they were the living, and also lyrical, language of restlessness and dissent. One stands in a peculiarly intimate relation to a poet, and even perhaps to a philosopher, whose work develops in parallel with one's own experience. A two-way running commentary is established, and one is either grateful to the poet for expressing what needs to be expressed at the right time, or one is censorious because he has failed to rise to some occasion (unknown to him), and because he has perversely taken a path of his own and failed to understand what was expected of him.

Mr. Auden has always left his followers behind. Not least in the Preface to the carefully prepared and revised collection of shorter poems[1], he looks back to his own public history in a disclaiming spirit, with a mild and elderly gaze and with some surprise. He seems to dislike some of the ungentlemanly opinions and political prophecies in his early verse, and he has repudiated the untidy involvements of the Thirties. But having been, for good reasons, the poet laureate of one dishevelled generation, at least in England, and having so far found no successor in full possession of the title, he cannot now easily slip away into an eccentric privacy, even if he is no longer representative and is no longer a public voice.

The original reasons for his dominance are not too difficult to understand. It seemed that in his poetry he never allowed fine fictions and believable truths to be divided only by a blurred and disputed line. He wanted always to be strictly truthful. For a generation made literal-minded by new political brutalities and by the probability of war, it was no longer possible to give licence to half-serious beliefs which seemed poetic playthings and which, taken by themselves, were just in-

[1] *Collected Shorter Poems*, 1927–1957. Faber, 1966.

credible. The whole apparatus of spell-binding and critical mystery, of hints and ironies, of allusions to Church and State, in Eliot's magnificent middle manner suddenly seemed to many heavy-handed and irrelevant. The vulgar, obvious questions had been carefully kept in the background for too long: can I believe a word–a magnificent word–of what the poet is indirectly saying? Must I care for the integrated society, for poetry's sake? So much reverence, so much disdain of contemporary thought and experience, and so much fine Bradleyan philosophy, disguised as criticism, had sooner or later to yield to plain speaking.

Mr. Auden was never reverent. Conjuring tricks with thought and language were left in his verse to look just like conjuring tricks. When he cast a sudden spell in his famous opening lines, he at the same time adopted the pose of the magician, undeceived. When he juggled with his beliefs, Marxist or Freudian, the jugglery depended upon metrical exuberance, upon a delight in verbal traps and in figures of speech and in imaginary landscapes. Whatever the play with his lyrical flights, it was open and aboveboard. So, following in the wake of the grand old pretenders, he seemed immensely modest, direct, and without pretences.

> . . . *It's as well at times,*
> *To be reminded that nothing is lovely,*
> *Not even in poetry, which is not the case.*

Perhaps most new turns in poetry, which capture a strong allegiance, have this aspect of a new literalness, of the restoration of poetry to a common light, and of kicking away of stilts. A hard intelligence which respects contemporary realities restores the authority of poetry, at least for a time. One is grateful for the speaking voice, for a closing of the gap between reader and writer, and for an easier tolerance of common concerns. After the grand old men, the soothsayers and oracles, Mr. Auden seemed the first of the post-modern writers in England, assimilating journalism, slogans, the slag-heaps and waste-matter of political minds, the boys' games and imaginary conspiracies of middle-class Englishmen, the jumbled notions of Freudian new thought, the decaying railway lines and semi-urban landscapes of Baldwin's England. He made poetry out of unmasked lies and mere propaganda, and, in *The Orators*, began a kind of literary pop art of his own which no one had seen before. He eliminated the Parnassian mode altogether, and borrowed the jerky rhythms and syncopations of musical comedy for the sake of a contrived vulgarity and catchiness, of a kind of anti-poetry. His lyrical gift was never used to justify a claim to a superior imaginative truth which cannot bear the test of prosaic doubt and of mere common sense. The moral didacticism is just left to show, undisguised, through his play with verse forms.

> *My problem is how not to will;*
> *They move most quickly who stand still;*
> *I'm only lost until I see,*
> *I'm lost because I want to be.*
>
> *If this should fail, perhaps I should,*
> *Content myself with this conclusion;*
> *In theory there is no solution.*
>
> *All statements about what I feel,*
> *Like I-am-lost, are quite unreal:*

My knowledge ends where it began;
A hedge is taller than a man.

In his didactic verse, the message is often mocked by the
manner, and he will see how thin, flat, and unpretending
he can be and still succeed. In other early poems, which
still seem as startling in their assurance and air of command
as when they were first read, the reminiscence of Yeats
is broken into fragments. The myths and esoteric philosophies have disappeared, and the imagery conveys
psychological truths, a diagnosis.

> '*I see the guilty world forgiven,*'
> *Dreamer and drunkard sing,*
> '*The ladders let down out of heaven,*
> *The laurel springing from the martyr's blood,*
> *The children skipping where the weeper stood,*
> *The rivers natural and the beasts all good.*'
>
> *So dreamer and drunkard sing;*
> *Till day their sobriety bring:*
> *Parrotwise with deaths reply;*
> *From whelping fear and nesting lie;*
> *Woods their echoes ring. . . .*

'From whelping fear and nesting lie'–this was the characteristic Auden topic. 'The Paysage Moralisé' became his
original style:

> *Hearing of harvests rotting in the valleys,*
> *Seeing at end of street the barren mountains,*
> *Round corners coming suddenly on water,*
> *Knowing them shipwrecked who were*
> *launched for islands,*

We honour founders of these starving cities,
Whose honour is the image of our sorrow.

This was the more or less political poetry of its time.

Look there! The sunken road winding
To the fortified farm.
Listen to the cock's alarm
In the strange valley.

Are we then the stubborn athletes;
Are we then to begin
The run between the gin
And bloody falcon?

The horns of the dark squadron,
Converging to attack;
The sound behind our back
Of glaciers calving.

As one reads to the end, 1927–1957, neither the mastery of verse forms nor the use of poetry as moral comment in an imaginary landscape seems greatly to change. The fact that many of the surviving early poems counted as politically inspired, and were written in the context of a supposed social revolution, seems to make little difference either to their meaning or their value. The Eden of congruity and justice that he constructs from disordered images of northern landscapes is the same all the way through, and the same kind of obsessional, or sacred, objects stand for sanity, order, and calm. Even when Mr. Auden turns most strongly, in his later verse, against political prophecy, and against political anxiety as a theme, one can still place a late poem among the earlier poems

and find no great unfittingness. He dominates his own
beliefs so completely that they seem never, or rarely, to
take him off his course, or to make him untrue to his own
temperament. In this respect he is, and intends to be, more
like an Augustan poet than any of his contemporaries.
The canons of good sense are already fixed, in the real and
obvious world, and he does not grope or flounder in his
published work. As far as a modern writer can, he has
made the idea of his own development seem critically
irrelevant. His development, he implies, is simply his
getting older, and must not be turned by his readers into
some exemplary spiritual progress, as if he were Goethe.
The famous poems of so many years ago –

> *Look, stranger, on this island now*
> *The leaping light for your light discovers,*

or:

> *As I walked out one evening*

or:

> *About suffering they were never wrong,*
> *The Old Masters . . .*

or 'Lullaby' or 'A Summer Night' – do not seem to be
exploratory, or to be a preparation for anything beyond
themselves. Nor do the more controlled and less ambitious
later poems, from the age of Empson, seem later poems.

> *Time will say nothing but I told you so,*
> *Time only knows the price we have to pay;*
> *If I could tell you I would let you know.*

If there is a discernible line of development at all, it is
simply that the proportion of song to epigram diminishes.

ABIGAIL E. WEEKS MEMORIAL LIBRARY
UNION COLLEGE
BARBOURVILLE, KENTUCKY

But even so one might not be able to guess whether these lines are late or early.

> *A sentence uttered makes a world appear*
> *Where all things happen as it says they do;*
> *We doubt the speaker, not the tongue we hear:*
> *Words have no word for words that are not true.*

Mr. Auden uses the discoveries of Blake, Lear, and Hardy, as well as of Yeats and Eliot, with a peculiar detachment. He takes the letter and experiments with it, and leaves the philosophical spirit behind. He returns to his predecessors, as a musician may, for the forms that they suggest to him for variation and development.

He is the first English poet, and one of the first major writers of any kind, whose way of thought has from the beginning been formed by an early knowledge of clinical psychology, and therefore by an amused understanding of the wild mechanisms of imagination. If Eliot sometimes seems a sidesman in a surplice, suspecting heresies, Mr. Auden's natural, and perhaps inherited, attitude is that of a clinician in a white coat, expecting epidemics of madness and hypochondria, the slow poisons that affect the whole political body and are natural disturbances of the mind. Anxiety, taken as a pathological symptom, is an unexpected theme for poetry, and he has made it his own. He is particularly the poet of the imaginary threat which becomes real, of a creeping political madness, of an epidemic of distraction and fear. One might crudely have expected that so much self-consciousness would undermine the power, and even the will, to invent. But it is characteristic of him to swerve from the most abstract and pedantic reflection to concrete imagery, and, in a sense, to swerve from prose to poetry within poetry. He likes to represent and to control panic by drawing up lists of its obsessional signs, and he sometimes uses poetry as an incantation that disinfects in a mocking spirit. He ensures that his own words are clean and that they carry no secondary infection of doubtful meanings.

So he has the habit of revising his earlier work, and one finds that familiar passages have disappeared. Any speck of mere poetic rhetoric which he has noticed has been removed. Like a philosopher of the analytical school, he does not want to be taken to mean more than he actually says, even by the narrowest margin; for he does not want to be an oracle, indeterminate in meaning. There cannot be both science and oracles or we shall be either mad or just frivolous, in the way that Yeats sometimes seemed frivolous, or at least half-serious, in assertion. If poetry and philosophy are different from the natural sciences and from religion, in their attitude to truth, the difference cannot be that they do not really mean what they seem to say.

Mr. Auden's attitude to poetical philosophizing is parallel to G. E. Moore's attitude to McTaggart, whom Yeats revered. If there is no literal sense in which Time is unreal, there ought to be no poetical or philosophical sense either, except as a pretence. If poetry is an intricate game, which, through an obsessional delight in formal rules, sometimes reveals hidden connections, the hidden connections must be there, visible even to a prosaic eye. If no hidden connections are discovered, or even attempted, poetry is just an intricate and absorbing game with images and signs, 'a contraption', a variant of nursery rhyme, or of song or nonsense verse; and so much the better: anything rather than literary egoism and home-made metaphysics. It is too late for these indulgences, which have in any case proved themselves insanitary and dangerous.

Mr. Auden has in recent years called for gentlemanly restraints upon men of letters who vulgarly claim too much for themselves. Whatever their eccentric skills, they know no more than they can rationally prove, and they have no sense that is superior to common sense and to the traditions of good manners and worldly prudence. They must not look for acknowledgment as legislators of the world; quixotism was finished, finally exposed, in the Thirties. A middle and modest style is appropriate to an age of fanaticism and of public indignities. Poetry may perhaps revive the virtues of the music of the eighteenth century, before the silly confusions (as he believes) between art and religion, or between art and ethics, began. It can illustrate a proper sense of scale and of measure, a respect for moderate moods, and a decent confinement of wild ambitions within clear and difficult forms. In his later writing, the anxiety and the hint of madness in the air, the sense of panic, that runs through the early verse can only be heard from much farther away. There is a natural aging in the collected editions of his verse and the poet is, as usual, entirely self-conscious about it.

The weight and variety of achievement are dazzling. The combination of lyricism and epigram, the controlled strangeness, the wit, the genius in formal invention, are a perpetual pleasure. He has become, and will surely remain, one of the most quotable of poets, typically, perhaps more in single verses and even phrases, rather than in whole poems. He seems often to be checking and curbing his own cleverness and his own artifices, in case they should go too far. He expresses, both in verse and in prose, a restrained and careful confidence in literature, kept in its proper place, which is on the surface of things. His most vivid writing refers to a natural order, a remembered landscape of suitable rock and soil and water, which are easily lost or spoiled now, as also when he was first published in Baldwin's England.

2

―◄ ►―

Letters of James Joyce

JOYCE was not, like Byron or Lawrence, a great letter-writer. It was no part of his design that he should be, and almost everything in his life, as in his work, was designed. He was to address posterity in nightspeech, and most of his letters are dayspeech. The principal topics are money, family arrangements, a constant search for places to live, censorship, publishers' evasions, limited editions, useful friends, and useful reviewers. There are a few elaborately composed letters, and there are undesigned moments. Most of these come early in his life and in his letter writing, before he had enclosed himself in his ark, over the flood of illness, poverty and European war. In a late letter in Italian to his son, Giorgio, he writes 'I opened the garret-window of my ark and see that the terraqueous world, and our six lives in particular, are in such a broth not to say dishwater'. The image of the ark is just. By this time events in the world beyond his family and his work, including the Second World War, are scarcely mentioned in his surviving letters. In his early years he had written to his brother, Stanislaus, about his soon extinguished allegiance to socialism, and also about his vast, already formed, ambitions. The surviving letters to Nora Barnacle during his courtship are of extraordinary, and sometimes even of sensational power. The violence and energy of his erotic imagination, the reckless concentration of his emotions, are so undisguised that the reader must

30

feel an awkward intruder, particularly if he goes to the original manuscript, to the yellowing pages in the neat scholar's handwiring. Not all the surviving early letters to Nora Joyce would be fittingly published. But some intimate letters to Nora have been published by Professor Ellmann, and they add substantially to that which may be learnt, and also inferred, from Professor Ellmann's biography.

Joyce could make it seem as if he and his wife were the only man and woman in existence, as if they were some mythical summation of humanity, and as if everything else around them was scenery on some dark stage upon which they alone stood in the light. This absoluteness and exclusiveness in his emotions, a blind man's singleness of mind, which can exclude the world, is of course a quality of his imagination at work also. From the letters one can see him wilfully forming for himself, from his earliest years, the architecture of the universally representative family: his father, John Stanislaus Joyce ('his voice somehow has got into my body or throat'), his mother early dead, his brother Stanislaus, his wife Nora, his son Giorgio, and daughter Lucia. Joyce will stand at the centre of the family, the representative hero, 'James the Punman', keeping at bay all the irrelevant world outside, and clearing a space for the fulfilment of his evident destiny; the evidence was in his name and heritage, as Irish artificer and demiurge, who would resume all the experience of all the families in his work. He will supervise his own biography, and insist that his biographer, Herbert Gorman, should fit his account of Joyce's relations with his father to the willed myth, which was half experience, and half literature. The necessary coherence of the family was his concern, in life as in literature, and not society. His early socialism left no residue, and, once having left Dublin, he was to live on the margins of settled society, moving from encampment to encampment, a proud mendicant, exacting a toll from his neighbours, but uncommitted to them, and ready to speak any European language familiarly, a 'street-singer', the wandering Irishman who would test the 'putrid social system' which does not recognise art. 'Without boasting I think I have little or nothing to learn from English novelists', he had written to his brother very early. How indeed could he have anything to learn from the traditions of the English novel, if he was to turn away altogether from the comedy of society, and of its changing forms in history, from the 'wideawake language, cutandry grammar, and goahead plot', in which awareness of social relations is naturally expressed? The nightspeech of the family is in all languages, or in his own single, fused, language; the same wife, father, son, daughter, brother, the same flowing feminine unpunctuated unsocialized consciousness speaks, with the same abundance of sexual imagery, in Clongowes, Dublin, Trieste, Paris, or Zürich. A European writer could come from a provincial margin of Europe, as Ibsen had also, bringing a new realism that would pass beneath the social crust, to the undifferentiated slime, the viscous prose, of the primary processes of thought. 'What is wrong with these English writers is that they always keep beating about the bush', he wrote to Stanislaus. They remain in the social daylight of consciousness, enclosed in a literal gentility, and the ready-made forms of their sentences, like frontiers on the map, segregate them from the truth of their interwoven memories and sexual dreams. Why should not a modern literature be as unsparing and direct as vulgar song?

Repeatedly in these letters one sees that for Joyce a singer was a sacred person, whether it was John Sullivan, whom he had adopted as an *alter ego*, or McCormack, or some member of his family; he liked to think of himself as a voice, Shame's Voice. The flow of a song may follow the river-bed of consciousness without conventional stops in settled meanings. Language also may flow, and follow the modulations of consciousness as he made it do, first and experimentally, in the conclusion of 'The Dead' in *Dubliners*. But language can flow freely, only on condition that the hard shell of the given word, and of the punctuated sentence, has been broken open, and the soft, associative core, set free. The singing, lilting language of Anna Livia Plurabelle can be a transparent voice from the page, with the dissolute meanings fading in and out, as each reader turns the voice on for himself. Late in his life, Joyce wrote in a letter of Dowland's Songs, in unique submission, 'I hope something I have written may bear comparison with "Come Silent Night"'. All through these letters his exact musical memories recur to him, while literature is mentioned less and less as he grows older in the solitude of his own work, and in the struggle for money, publication, and independence. He did not need anyone else's writing, only the encouragement and help of writers. Yeats, Eliot, and, above all, Mr. Ezra Pound, gave their encouragement and help. Mr. Pound appears in these letters, once again, as the untiring, absolutely disinterested and honest defender of Joyce's genius almost from the beginning; his help was almost as indispensable as that of Harriet Shaw Weaver, Adrienne Monnier, and Sylvia Beach. He was evidently at ease with Joyce's pride and pose and with his harshness; he was bored by *Finnegans Wake*, but he always helped.

The Shem and Shaun story told in Stanislaus Joyce's *My Brother's Keeper* comes occasionally to the surface here, particularly in the earlier letters. Joyce demanded his attention; Stanislaus was the brother as designated listener, and he was to be the messenger to and from the normal world for normal readers. 'What is the meaning of that rout of drunken words [*Finnegans Wake*]? It seems to me pose, the characteristic that you have in common with Wilde, Shaw, Yeats, and Moore.' In this letter Stanislaus strikes one side of the Irish truth, as Joyce himself portrays it in the conscious swagger of many of his own letters, as also in the person of Stephen in *Ulysses*. He is a giant and a satyr, rioting among small men in the field of European language, while Shaw and the others 'beat about the bush', content to amuse the public on its own terms. Joyce will begin a literature that is like a pub brawl of oaths and puns and remembered snatches of song from the competing drunken voices of ten or more languages. The truth of a common consciousness is scrawled in graffiti, layer upon layer upon the walls of the mind, a jumble of half-forgotten names and misspellings and obscenities, a condensation of everyman's dreams, already songs for the blind street-singer, who from a distance away hears shouting and mumbling and quarrelling voices along the river, at the night-time closing. This listening to, and reforming of, snatches and cadences of voices was not pose, but his 'individual passion' naturally expressed even in informal letters. The pose, of which Stanislaus complained, was rather in the will to completeness: every possible pun, Dublin scene, significant date and memory, should somewhere be given its place in the final book, which would astonish, exhaust, and finally subdue any possible reader. 'Is it possible that, after all, men of letters are no more than entertainers?' Joyce had asked in a letter as early as 1905; the thought, provoked by reading Goldsmith, was unbearable to him. His own work should be a monument to the absence of the desire to please. 'The struggle against conventions in which I am at present involved was not entered into by me so much as a protest against these conventions as with the intention of living in conformity with my moral nature.' In his claim for the autonomy of the artist, he would take one step beyond Flaubert, beyond *Bouvard et Pécuchet*, shielded by a stony detachment from the reader's impertinence. 'If it is not farfetched to say that my action, and that of men like Ibsen, is a virtual intellectual strike, I would call such people as Gogarty and Yeats and Colm the blacklegs of literature' (1906). They, like Wilde, are the Irish performers, the comedians who trail their personalities before the public, and who serve the old Anglo-Saxon 'idols' at a lower rate for the job. Joyce would withdraw his labour from the market for literary entertainment, and *Finnegans Wake* was his prolonged rebellion.

Once the gesture had been made, and the way to an autonomous literature marked out, Joyce could suggest that someone else might complete the work for him. The suggestion was impossible for many reasons, but principally because the mania for completeness, and the obsession with coincidences, were inimitable peculiarities of Joyce's own imagination, and are apparent already in the early letters. He had a superstitious sense of the sacredness of coincidence, particularly of the coincidence of a name or of a date, which could confer an occult meaning on trivial facts. Some of his work can be seen as a vast refinement of bog-Irish superstition, which would find epiphanies in the rearrangement of the most drab facts. He was a free-thinking sacramentalist, who dabbled in the occult, which Vico had prefigured as the verbal occult. No one else would mind his meanings, share his willed superstitions, and unravel his doomsday oracles and black humours. With their aid he drove almost everyone away, even at times Nora Joyce, with unconditional demands on their loyalty, as on the loyalty of his readers. 'What I want to wear away in this novel [*A Portrait of the Artist*] cannot be worn except by constant dripping.' 'Wearing away' was his method also in living and with people. Not once in these letters is he seen to make any unhumorous concession to his own poverty, weariness, illness, and loneliness, or to the weaknesses of anyone else. His fortitude was absolute and unyielding.

The letters have been published discontinuously: a first volume was published in 1957 by Mr. Stuart Gilbert, and Professor Ellmann's two volumes count as the second and third volumes of the complete set, although they include many of the earliest letters. Professor Ellmann prints more than two hundred letters to Joyce, and many of them, and particularly Nora Joyce's, throw light on the fiction. As usual, one finds that there is a closer relation between the fiction and the autobiographical facts than one had supposed. Nora and May Joyce did write, in their rôles as wife and mother, with a flowing simplicity which corresponds to Joyce's renderings of the universal feminine consciousness. It is as if they are singing their arias in the opera which Joyce had composed from his life.

Like Ibsen again, he needed his own picture of a distinct feminine consciousness; for him it was necessary that women in the family should be a gentle chamber music, enveloping, unfettered, forgiving, life-continuing, and also that the circean brothel, a route of obscenities, should always be open for his goat-dance, for a running farce of antic couplings, which are a kind of sexual misspelling, a defiance of the grammar of human relations, fixed forever in the family. Professor Ellmann brilliantly interprets some of the bafflement, and a sense of emptiness, which a reading of Joyce may sometimes leave when he writes: 'The method of his prose books is a kind of absorption of the universe rather than a facing up to it: he seems to draw it bit by bit inside him, and conceives of the imagination as a womb.' Joyce himself wrote to his son in Italian in 1935: 'My eyes are tired. For over half a century they have gazed into a nullity where they have found a lovely nothing.' All his work is retrospect and memory, written from inside the ark of his own designs.

The prolonged agony of his many eye operations, and the even greater agony of his daughter's mental illness, dominated his later years. He thought that he was responsible for Lucia's mental collapse, and he struggled with all his wild tenacity to find a cure. It is a terrible story, and for once even his bitter gaiety was overwhelmed. He became more than ever like Job, who was the inventor of the interior monologue. Having step by step overcome poverty and blindness, and the censorship that barred his way to publication, and having achieved at last recognition and fame, he died amidst sadness and with this one defeat. But he knew that he was a first founder of the modern movement in prose writing.

3

━◄►━

Virginia Woolf

IT is difficult to guess, more than thirty-five years after *The Waves* was published (1931), how slight or how strong the hold of Virginia Woolf upon contemporary readers may still be. 1931 was a year of catastrophe: *Between the Acts* appeared in 1941 in an even greater blackness. Reading these novels as they appeared, one did not doubt that one was watching an extension of English literature, an addition to the resources of the language, which might have no consequences, but which would never be forgotten. For me, as probably for many Englishmen, these two novels, and *To the Lighthouse* as well, are not easily separated from the setting in which they first appeared. Together with the poetry and prose of the later Eliot, of Auden, Isherwood, and Spender, they belong to that brilliant pre-war phase of English experimental writing. They recall the disappointed enthusiasms of the Popular Front and intellectuals protesting against Fascism. Virginia Woolf was a contributor, on at least one occasion, to the *Daily Worker*; there was a splendour in this incongruity, even if the episode marked principally the desperation of that time.

Now there is surely time to think again about her achievement, away from the local prejudices which, at least in England, have absurdly concealed some of the true qualities of her genius. Some of the dominant academic critics in England have for many years parroted phrases about the Bloomsbury Group, and smothered her work with nervous polemics. Her elaborate play with language in her lighter works, and as a critic and journalist, seems to have aroused a sense of social grievance among critics, because her tone and style were taken to be a return to a genteel tradition of *belles-lettres*, which should have been discredited. A remoteness, a bookishness, a conscious poise and cultivation of literary manner in the widely read *The Common Reader* established a public character which obscured, at least for a time, her deeper purposes as a novelist.

Jean Guiguet, author of 'Virginia Woolf and her Works', is far away from these vagaries of English opinion. He is well aware that *A Writer's Diary*, as edited by Leonard Woolf, can only tell a very small part of the story, and that most of the biographical sources, particularly letters, are still missing. So great is his enthusiasm and respect that he sometimes attributes to Virginia Woolf virtuous intentions which it is very unlikely she would have had. She was uncompromisingly aristocratic in her attitudes: she despised many things, and worthy academic criticism was one of them. She admired wit, recklessness, and the crushing intellectual arrogance with which she had been familiar all her life. As a Frenchman, he looks for, and finds, a philosophical thesis in the novels, which he expresses in abstract words that might not have greatly interested her. But this is a solid and serious book, without any of the now dreaded affectation and apparatus of so much Anglo-Saxon criticism.

I suppose that this apparatus of modern criticism, which is not mere reviewing or journalism, has the same function as the apparatus of the law courts: to preserve the dignity and distance of the critic's judicial office. The critic, unlike the reviewer, must be defended against the risk of seeming unbalanced, arbitrary, too personal, too partial in the selection of evidence; he must not be caught in the act of rigging the evidence to satisfy his own emotional responses. I do not pretend to be judicial, to sum up points for and against, when this entirely original, uneven, and occasionally great, writer is in question. It will always be easy to gather evidence for a dismissive verdict against Virginia Woolf; her writing can become arch and trivial and weakly decorative (as in *Three Guineas*); her ambitions can fail to acquire substance, the effect can be papery and thin and cold (as in some parts of *Mrs. Dalloway* and in *The Years*), and the characters unrealized, except as vehicles for the author's virtuosity. Her own words for her defects were 'watery and flimsy and pitched in too high a voice', and these words do apply to her weaker work and even to some passages in *To the Lighthouse*. The negative evidence can be piled up, if a balanced verdict is desired. But the point and the pleasure will be missed; once the sharp edge and strangeness of her genius have been felt, and separated from the surface impression, she can be found one of the most unsettling and poignant writers of her time, who penetrated to levels of experience and of feeling which are not explored elsewhere. She describes 'the world seen without a self', the ordinary madness that lies, as she believed, just beneath the solid world of unperceiving sanity.

The impression that her finest writing, and particularly her two masterpieces, *The Waves* and *Between the Acts*, conveys is of a wildness and violence below a hard and beautiful surface which scarcely contains them; it is as if a whirling confusion, a horror of chaos and of disintegration, is just being kept at a distance. The characters hold on to conventional reality, but they know that they are clinging to a frail convention only. Along the path of their nerves, and in their unguarded perceptions, they continually receive intimations of another and more primitive world, in which solid objects dissolve, lose their shape and coherence, become threatening or enchanting, and leave a trail of unexplored significances; the colours and rhythms are more insistent, and at this deeper level gloom and brightness are juxtaposed, as in a jungle, and the most humdrum objects are swept from their placid English setting in some breaking wave of primary emotion. The speakers in *The Waves* feel a kind of anguish in sensation, as they struggle to hold the world steady; it is slipping away from their grasp. Their friends, and the occasion of their meeting, the hurrying moment, will not be fixed, and those rounded presences, real people, cannot quite be realized and held in focus. A true consciousness is more rapid than we must conventionally pretend, and once opened and uncontrolled, will run in ecstasy from the pattern in the tablecloth to the pattern of meetings and absences among friends. The agony of loss in *The Waves* is as much the loss of a moment, of an unusual instant of true communication, arrested and perfect, a point of intersection between monologues, as it is the loss of a friend who has died. Only in the practice of an art can one both suspend the reality principle, and allow the gross facts of time-governed reality to dissolve before one's eyes, and yet retain a sense of identity, a continuing sanity. So Virginia Woolf wrote of herself in her Diary: '. . . something very profound about the synthesis of my being: how only writing composes it: how nothing makes a whole unless I am writing';

and again, 'Odd how the creative power at once brings
the whole universe to order'. Words allow the whirling
chaos to be recognized, to be placated, to be contained and
formed; the violent rhythms of anguish and exaltation can
be realized in free imagery, and the English language, the
language of Sterne and of the Elizabethans, can match
the pace of a dissociated sensibility. She wrote, and her
characters speak, with the fear of madness near to them.
But the painful magic of sentences and phrases can gather
the distracted fragments of a personality together, and
give it a shape, and a sense of identity. The saving phrases
echo along the corridors of perception from childhood,
and carry a magical meaning.

The quest for reality explains the changing form of the
novels. Narrative is that form of description which must
be unfaithful to *l'expérience vécue*. We need a form of
fiction which, like Emily Brontë's, 'could free life from
its dependence on facts'. Obituaries must lie; this was, for
Virginia Woolf, a necessary, and not a contingent, truth.
Perceptions always carry unnamed emotions, and no true
story can be told without the flow of perceptions, the
subject's temporary world, which he does not control at
will. So a style and a form are needed that 'transmit emotion without impediment', give a luminous immediacy
of impression, without the scaffolding of exposition and
plot, which must break the flow. The post-impressionist
painters, whom Roger Fry admired, had liberated themselves from conventions of representation, and had found
a new immediacy by suppressing all explanatory transitions, bridge passages, inert segments of the canvas that
are mere picture-building; this analogy was certainly in
Virginia Woolf's mind.

But neither the motive nor the value of her writing is to be found in these abstract and methodological concerns, cherished by the new Cartesians in France, who have almost buried Virginia Woolf beneath their doctoral philosophizings. 'Le roman psychologique', with the inevitable allusions to Dujardin and Joyce, is an irrelevance. The personal urgency and the density of feeling in *The Waves* disappear in an analysis of this abstract kind. The bleak conclusion of this line of criticism is to be found in Nathalie Sarraute's patronage of Virginia Woolf in *The Age of Suspicion*. Mlle Sarraute wholly detaches the method from the substance, as if novels, whether written by Proust or by Butor or by Virginia Woolf, were all directed towards the same subject matter, but employed different methods to reach it; just as in biology there could be mechanists and vitalists, so there can be psychologizing novels, now shown to be mistaken and superseded, and objective novels, now the approved rational method. This pretence that 'The Novel', or 'The Modern Novel', is a continuing inquiry into some independently recognized problem, and is therefore akin to philosophy, is particularly misleading here. Virginia Woolf knew very well that her visions of the reality behind appearances were partial and eccentric, that Rhoda and Neville and Jinny in *The Waves* lived among strange, rare, enclosing images and perceptions. She knew also that her perceptions must be more violent and threatening than those of other writers, reverberating along nerves that were more taut, and scattering in wild discords, uncontrolled at the centre: that for her 'nothing makes a whole', as it would for Tolstoy or Thackeray. The immediacy for which she struggled was an immediacy in the transmission of primary emotion, unfocused upon enduring objects: of the literally overwhelming sense of the strangeness of being alive, of the horror of an inner darkness, like a tunnel of fear, as the sense of identity disintegrates: in her words, 'the sensation of all the violence and unreason crossing in the air: ourselves small: a tumult outside: something terrifying'. In *Kew Gardens*, in some passages of *To the Lighthouse*, throughout *The Waves* and *Between the Acts*, the hurrying menace of disembodied emotion, like the drumming of horses' hooves, or the pounding of waves on the shore, is insistently present in the tense writing. Her men and women hold on, sometimes despairingly, to some solid centre, to some handrail over the chaos of the whirling sensations, which form their dissolving patterns. In love and in friendship there can be, temporarily, 'a riveting together of the shattered fragments of the world'. But they are threatened, and haunted, by the memory of an unendurable loss: the loss of a brother, or, later, of a friend, which had once shattered 'the little strip of pavement over an abyss'—Virginia Woolf's picture of her own experience. The small group of friends, in *The Waves*, which, biographically, may be seen as a reflection of a Cambridge coterie and of Bloomsbury, was more significantly a representation of 'the little strip of pavement over the abyss', a linking around Percival, the solidly upright male figure at the centre, who had held the common, man-made world of fact together, but who is dead.

It could be said that this beautiful novel is too static and emotionally stifling, and that the dismissal of bodily presences and of actual events is unbearable as fiction, because it seems pathological; or that the whole work is 'too egotistical', the author's own verdict on some of her work. It may be too egotistical, in the sense that the immediacy, which she had so long sought, removes an essential condition of fiction; the author's emotions are transmitted without resistance along the nerves of her prose, and the reader may be left helpless, either overwhelmed or repelled, and in either case without the independent material on which his imagination can begin to work. The implications are already stated, and the novel criticizes itself. The resources of the language are magnificently stretched; there is nothing else in English literature that resembles *The Waves* in its attempt to render very general, even cosmic, emotions by a controlled profusion of images, concrete, various, and exact. No one else has used language with this extravagance and yet kept a hardness of surface at the same time. *The Waves* has, as a novel, the virtues of a great Fauve painting, a celebration in bright colours of the emotions of raw vision and of a too unshuttered awareness, and is similarly disciplined. After the luxury and the beauty of the language, 'a great sense of the brutality and wildness of the world' remains with the reader, and, on any re-reading, the apparent preciosity of the material disappears in this sense of ecstasy, loneliness, and loss, so thrown into relief. The novel does render 'all the insanity of personal existence' and those characteristic moments of 'sudden transparencies', when 'the walls of the mind grow thin'.

Between the Acts, which Virginia Woolf considered 'more quintessential', is a turning away from egotism and subjectivity, and, though unrevised, seems to me flawless, and in need of no defence at all against hostile critics. It is a wonderfully compressed story, as clear on its surface as in its themes; during the single summer day described, the pageant of a contracting England drags on, too slowly, towards the evening, and masks the gradual overcoming of despair. The wildness and violence in the too bland air are at last given a name and a substance, at least in part, as sexual love and estrangement, and as the blind, natural force that holds people together when the voices stop, and the common history is forgotten, and when Miss La Trobe goes away, alone, knowing that her art cannot altogether be heard, or finally understood. She is a feminine, or half-feminine, unmagical, muttering Prospero, who in her art attempts the impossible, and who is heard only in snatches. In the worst year of the war, only 'a wedge-shaped core of darkness' ahead, this novel seemed an epitaph; literature would be carried forward almost into the night, as the bourgeois world faded and dispersed, with the story of that particular phase of English history told and concluded. All that can be done with words to ward off death and destruction—and the effort was half a failure and half a success—has been done, and it is time to go. Life would be renewed, primitively, in the night, and Miss La Trobe, alone in her pub, would have no part in this renewal. It was difficult in 1941 to read the story in any other way. But the story, and Miss La Trobe, now seem to have a more various and lasting beauty and a less simple suggestiveness. This last novel may be small in scale; but like any great work of art, it can be read again in different ways at different times. Around the walls of the mind, which had grown too thin, a fortification had finally been built in a work which was no longer egotistical. But Virginia Woolf had been exhausted by the headlong pursuit of a controlling form, and died in the River Ouse.

4

E. M. Forster

A N underlying argument, a division of allegiance, runs
through all of Mr. Forster's writing and shapes the
developing style and structure of his novels. Roughly
stated, the division is between, on the one side, an inherited
liberalism, confirmed among philosophical friends at Cambridge and never altogether discarded, which stressed
the authority of the individual conscience, and stressed also
the qualities of sensitiveness and lucidity in personal relations within the setting of a civilized private life. On
the other side, Mr. Forster has always represented the
natural order surrounding this little compound of cultivated ground as sublime, unknown, unlimited, and as
not adapted to our powers of understanding. We cannot
be safe and at home within the compound, however much
we may defensively pretend to be. One function of art is
to take men outside the compound of conscious awareness,
beyond their moral anxieties, and to find expression for
the deeper rhythms in nature from which we are otherwise
disconnected. This is one implication of the often-quoted
Forster aphorism 'only connect', which has a philosophical
rather than a social sense. The connection that needs to be
made is between the upper and literate reaches of the mind
and the lower and unwashed, or proletarian, levels of
consciousness, which can no longer be downtrodden and
despised; for they are ready to strike back, and to withdraw their energies, if they are not accepted and set free.

There was a kind of provincialism in the enlightened and entirely secular thought which had developed among Mr. Forster's contemporaries at Cambridge in the generation that succeeded Mill and Sidgwick. In the more or less secret society of the Apostles in Cambridge, to which Mr. Forster naturally belonged, a new intellectual life was founded on the probing of meanings and the rejection of mysteries. Keynes described in *Two Memoirs* the sudden illumination which G. E. Moore's analytical philosophy had brought to the society and to the generation at Cambridge directly and indirectly formed by it. A lucid consciousness, the willed and curious enjoyment of love and friendship and of aesthetic emotions, were taken to be the proper themes of morality, and correspondingly, of that conversation among friends which develops into literature. This new self-consciousness must inform any literature that would interest a generation for whom Christianity, and indeed any transcendental philosophy, were no longer worthy of discussion. Now the degree of truthfulness and of clarity which can be achieved in the inner consciousness of individuals is alone worth exploring. Only states of mind, cultivated, observed, and authentically discriminated, could have value, as G. E. Moore had taught, in a natural order that is otherwise inert and neutral; neutral, that is, except in so far as it may give rise to aesthetic emotions, which must themselves be analysed, understood, and purged of sentimental irrelevancies. Fiction, no less than Roger Fry's art criticism, must serve that clear consciousness, which is the ability to articulate and make distinct the dim repulsions and attractions, naturally felt, which conventional minds are afraid to distinguish and to name. The value is to be found

in the distinguishing, in the letter that you write or in the
account that you can give among friends, in the analysis
of experience, of its precise form and nature, rather than
in the dumb promptings and confusions of experience
itself. If you always know what you mean, you are saved;
you belong to the true gentry of the mind, who are at
home in their gardens and in command of the natural
sources of feeling. If enlightened men are placed in nature,
as in a garden, and on cultivated ground, the point must
be to know the names of the plants, to botanize among the
emotions, to stroll with one's secateur, snipping the buds
in talk. One is to forget about the wilderness of unfenced
feeling outside; because it is undistinguished and un-
labelled, there can be nothing of real interest there.

These are images from Mr. Forster's earlier novels,
which have the delicacy of being composed from within
the assumptions that they implicitly question. He used the
traditional forms of social comedy, and made his stories
turn at their crisis on a failure of articulateness, a weakness
in distinguishing clearly, on the unpardonable clumsiness
of not saying what one really means. Yet he used these
familiar forms in *Howard's End* and in *The Longest Journey*
to suggest by an added resonance of style, particularly
in natural description, that the values of an inner truthfulness and of lucidity of feeling were very incomplete; they
can no longer be wholeheartedly accepted, as they had
been by Jane Austen, to whose thought and purpose the
forms of social comedy were perfectly appropriate. He
sometimes conveys his aims by an analogy with music
forms. He would write about a house and a family's
relation to it, about gentility and social distinctions and
marriage, about the self-consciousness that may corrupt

those who do good, and at the same time indicate that these are not really to be taken as his central themes, as they may be in *Emma*. The social tensions also convey a philosophical conflict. His method was to hint at this conflict, and his art was an art of allusion. The allusion was to the inadequacy of the ethics of a clear consciousness and of a civilized private life, which places the human intelligence at the centre of the universe, as the unique source of value and of significance.

By virtue of this philosophical doubt Mr. Forster has generally been included within the modern movement. His early novels appeared to be a forewarning of what was to come, the beginning of the end of the nineteenth-century novel in England. It is difficult now to make the anxious operations of an individual's conscience the centre of interest in fiction, as Henry James still could, without implying some wider setting. A story that unfolds within the four walls of a house, within a settled and customary privacy, will now be lent some exemplary meaning, social or philosophical, of which the imagined personal relations are only an emblem. Some of the experiments of the modern movement in literature can be attributed to the undermining of the ethics of secular liberalism, of the belief in the final value and interest of the individual case. If one asks why *The Longest Journey* seems on the surface, perhaps most of all in America, remote in style from contemporary sensibility, the answer is to be found in the type of moral preoccupation that gives substance to the plot. Can salvation and admission to the company of the elect be found by enlightenment alone and by emancipation from the cold conventions of the north? These are issues drawn from the heyday of advancing liberal thought, alive and intense in *Middlemarch*. It is the interest of Mr. Forster's writing, extending from 1902 until the present day, that he is a bridge between the ethical culture of the nineteenth century in England and the modern movement, which was typified for Forster by Lawrence. With the sole exception of the last pages of *A Passage to India*, Mr. Forster has kept to the traditional forms and has not defied the ordinary canons of taste and credibility, as Lawrence did in his effort to break away from the ethics of individual responsibility, and from the depiction of managed emotions, fully understood and expressed. Forster's novels may therefore have sometimes seemed apart from, and irrelevant to, the main stream, an island of peaceful and traditional accomplishment. But the appearance is deceiving. All through his writing there is a tension, a productive muddle in thought and artistic aim. How seriously can moral earnestness, the earnest dissent of Mill and Sidgwick, and even of Mr. Forster's friends at Cambridge, be taken? Has it become a vulgar illusion to suppose that nature as a whole has laboured to produce, as its final triumph and justification, the sensitive individual conscience? Is humanism, taken as the assumption that consciousness is the measure of all things, a defensive conceit, which is horribly exposed as soon as one is far away from Surrey and the Home Counties? Are there attractions and repulsions and ambiguous energies which cannot be too finely examined and understood, but which can only be indirectly expressed? These are broad philosophical questions which are raised again and again in Forster's fiction from the earlier stories, with their unassimilated elements of fantasy, to the last definitive work.

In *A Passage to India* the implied metaphysics is at last

embodied in the story, not apologetically added in the guise of fantasy, as in the earlier stories, or sentimentally disguised, as in *The Longest Journey* and *Where Angels Fear to Tread*. The scale is finally the right one for the vision, which places the anxious human beings, for the first time fully realized and memorable characters, against the immense, subduing background of the subcontinent, the Temple, the Mountain, and the Cave. The protagonists in *A Passage to India* seem to be more honestly and solidly presented by the author just because he is at the same time absorbing them into his larger design. In *The Longest Journey* and *Howard's End* there is a nagging impression of falsity, which shows principally in the invocation of naturalness, as if Mr. Forster with an unavowed fastidiousness despised his characters, and particularly the women, for the finiteness and smallness of their ends, and therefore by implication despised his own story. Unlike Jane Austen, he could find no excitement of self-discovery in the act of marriage, in finding a place in society, as the climax of a story which leaves no loose ends dangling. Precisely the loose ends, the intermediate and unrecognized connections, interested him, as they were to interest Lawrence. Their imaginations were concerned with the undifferentiating flood rather than with the entry, two by two and segregated, into the Ark. The social framework in which, in these early stories, we view love and friendship and marriage is too neat and belittling, because it seems to put human discrimination at the centre, when in fact there is no centre, or, if there is, we cannot know where it is. The question that Mr. Forster has always implied is: 'Will it really profit us so much if we save our souls and lose the whole world?'

The perception of wholeness is in question. Integrity, a hard separateness, can be achieved only by a contraction of the sympathies that might connect us with parts of the world that are remote from our own. From one point of view, it might have been better for the English in India to speak less clearly, to blurt and stammer more, and to enter into those sudden quarrels and bursts of affection among their Indian friends which they did not allow themselves to understand. The integrity of the individual administrator or doctor, and the self-respect founded on it, kept the tiny English minority in India upright while also keeping them apart, unconnected. *A Passage to India* shows why that whole world was soon to be lost. Mrs. Moore discovers that she has the virtue of a rock rather than that of a sponge, and is shattered. Mr. Forster makes one feel both sides of this particular opposition as no other writer has. He understands perfectly the tight, fastidious accents of the English middle classes, as they used to be, and the trimmed hedges of their emotions, with the debris swept away as 'nerves'. He understands the fear of being absorbed into the surrounding country, of losing distinctness and control, and of surrendering to intimations of fulfilment that cannot be analysed and accounted for. Integrity requires that one should not allow music, or any work of art, to sweep over one and to carry one away, until it has first justified itself as properly constructed and intelligible; as in aesthetics, so also in the relations between the races, and especially in sexual relations, distinctness and a definite labelling of differences should be preserved.

Mr. Forster's mythical pantheism, and his belief that a confused and inarticulate consciousness may often be a

better guide to the realities, leaves him to imitate, sometimes awkwardly, finally successfully, in the construction
of *A Passage to India*, the unassertive suggestiveness of
music, while still preserving the most literal forms of
narrative. He has not only required of the reader a common
understanding of the social implications of his story, but
also a sympathy with the inarticulate ups and downs of
sexuality and of fear below the levels of consciousness,
conveyed in the texture of the writing. He found in the
visual art of India and in Indian thought a vindication of
the sources of his own distrust of liberal humanism, of its
pretensions to a willed lucidity and order. The profusion
and extravagance of forms and of sexual variety were a
rebuke to the optimism of doctrines of self-knowledge.
The doctrines of relaxed will and of the superior honesty
of unmoralized feeling; the belief in the deeper significance
of music among the arts, and of Indian art, with its cele-
brations of unrestricted sexuality: these form a pattern
and represent a temperament which was converted by
Schopenhauer into a philosophy. For Mr. Forster they
were one side of a conflict which can be interpreted at
different levels, as at once a social conflict and a philosophical one. Philosophically, the issue concerns the scale
on which the characters, British and Indian, see themselves against the background of India and its monuments.
The British ride across the vast landscape with a self-
importance that is inseparable from their clear purpose,
their respect for the sanctity of individual life and for
man-made justice. They hold themselves apart from the
unmeasured licence, the teeming births and deaths outside
the compound, and from the uncalculated renewals of
Indian life, which are the basis of a different dignity. Out-

side the compound men accept their immersion in inhuman processes that have their own uncalculated justice and balance, plotted on a different time scale. The story of the national and social misunderstanding and disconnectedness, fascinating in itself, is a fitting sign of the meeting of the two philosophical attitudes.

Since *A Passage to India* Mr. Forster has published no more novels. His vision had been expressed, and the bridge built: a bridge, among other things, between two periods and two styles in English fiction.

5

Sade

CONSISTENT theories, consistently held and practised, are apt to make dull fiction. 'I am a philosopher', Sade wrote of himself, and, if allowance is made for the pre-Kantian sense of the word, the claim is not absurd.[1] He early formed, and never later doubted, a general theory of Nature, and of human nature, and he deduced his principles of conduct and of art from this theory. The absence of doubt, the unwavering literal consistency, have left his novels and stories among the curiosities of literature, lumps of propaganda, illustrations of theory, like the works of the later social realists. Young girls roasting on a spit like chickens under the eyes of libertines are uninteresting, at least as characters in fiction. There is too little ambiguity in their situation, too little play for imagination in interpreting it. But the philosophical theory so illustrated is not irrelevant, and it has been responsibly examined by Camus, and by others, as a doctrine of individual liberty, without the shadow of any necessary compromise.

The two starting-points of Sade's original philosophy were not in themselves original: first, an angry atheism. Outside the order of Nature there is nothing to be known or desired, feared or respected.

The existence of a Creator is a revolting absurdity
. . . I have no need whatsoever to curb my leanings

[1] Gilbert Lély, *The Marquis de Sade*. Elek, 1961.

56

with the aim of pleasing him. Nature granted these urges to me, and to resist them would be to outrage it . . . In Nature's hands I am only a piece of mechanism that nature moves as it will, and there is not one of my crimes but serves it.

Secondly, Sade was a thoroughgoing determinist.

Our behaviour does not depend on ourselves, but on our make-up, our organization . . . One cannot give oneself virtues, nor is one any longer able to adopt this or that taste, any more than a hunchback can make himself straight. . . . That is my permanent view of life and I shall never give it up.

Helvétius, Holbach, and La Mettrie, and the other enthusiasts of Enlightenment, were also professed determinists, looking forward to an exact moral science that would enable us to plan for human happiness. But Sade's belief in determinism was not primarily a belief in a project of reform, or in a possible moral science. It was also the recognition of a present fact of experience, and this recognition directly guided his personal life. 'When the science of anatomy is perfected, it will be easy by its means to show the relation between man's inner organization and the urges which move him.' How foolish the judges, moralists, and executioners will appear at that time. Sade exults in their foolishness. They have misconceived the subject-matter on which they dare to pronounce, but which they do not dare to analyse in their own persons.

From such a harsh materialism it might seem that no ends of action could be inferred. A 'piece of mechanism' does not choose its own motions. But Sade found a positive value in setting the whole intricate mechanism to work, in realizing experimentally all the contradictory impulses that Nature had implanted in him. Only Nature merits respect and constitutes any kind of superior sanction. Our need is to uncover its secret operations–secret, because they have been concealed by cowards.

> People just do not conceive how essential these pictures [in Sade's writing] are to the development of man's heart. If we are still so ignorant about this matter, this is only due to the stupid restraint of those who choose to write on such matters. Entrammelled by ridiculous fears, all they discuss are childish things that any fool knows, and they are afraid to thrust a fearless hand into the human heart and to show us what monstrously wild things it is capable of.

This looks like an ethics of honesty and of truthfulness. But it is also something more.

All the philosophers of the Enlightenment believed that freedom depended on living in accordance with Nature, truthfully discovered. Sade's difference from them lay in his method of discovery. Hume, and the French philosophers of the Enlightenment, were content with a broad, synthetic treatment of human motives and passions, and with easy generalizations, which were not designed to penetrate the surface of observed behaviour or to disturb our ordinary classifications of the sentiments. Sade's method was analytical: 'You know,' he boasted, 'that nobody analyses as well as I do'. He had the idea of showing that, concealed behind the synthetic label of sexual instinct, there exists a great range of distinct impulses and emotions, peculiar to human beings and

58

unrelated to a single biological need. He therefore studied methodically, both in practice and in his writing, the varieties of sexual perversion, and the fantasies that accompany them.

He had taken three steps beyond any of his contemporaries. First, he assumed that the sexual impulses and emotions are the foundations of individual temperament and character. Secondly, he notices that in human beings the sexual impulses are originally polymorphous, and that socially recognized normality is only one specialization of sexual desire among many others. Thirdly, he believed that the primary impulses are ambivalent, and that the emotions of love and hatred, in any pure, unmixed form, are an artificial and precarious development of them. The artifice is never complete. In the natural and unregulated constitution of men, any intense desire to preserve the object of emotion is linked with an impulse to destroy it, any intense desire to please with the impulse to attack and to destroy. The non-logical, or contradictory, nature of men's original attachments Sade discovered for himself by probing his own consciousness, and by discarding civilized restraints.

Destructive impulses are an original element both in love and in self-love. Men not only seek pleasure and to preserve themselves, but, at the same time and in relation to the same objects, they seek pain and to destroy themselves. They only distort and smother their 'sensibility', their capacity for any intense feeling, when they try to hide these facts from themselves. They can be liberated by admitting the facts to full consciousness. Here Sade was a man of his time: to live as one should live is to live in accord with one's original Nature, and in an awakened enjoyment of its possibilities. But he separated this doctrine from the sentimental assumption, then prevailing, that Nature must present only harmonious possibilities, when they are rightly identified. On the contrary, he writes— 'Mark its ways, see what it does, Nature is frightful: you will never see it create but to destroy, never attain its ends but by murdering.' The picture is like De Maistre's, but he draws the opposite moral conclusion: not the need of absolute authority, but the need of absolute licence.

> Without the profound laws of balance, everything would be destroyed in the world. It is only by wrong-doing that Nature holds together . . . So when we abandon ourselves to evil, we are obeying Nature, and resistance would be the only crime that Nature could not forgive in us.

This Hegelian reversal of the prevailing picture of Nature is no less a mere picture, without scientific authority. But at least it exposes the vacuity of any consoling naturalism. The philosophers of the Enlightenment had presumed upon a too simple analogy between human sentiments and natural forces in physical things, imagining a science of human nature, parallel with Newton's physics. This assumption conveniently absolved them from any direct probing after more intimate self-knowledge. In the moral sciences we need only be detached, external observers of the gross regularities of human behaviour, as history has recorded them. Sade has recently been accepted as a serious figure in the history of thought, particularly in France, because he was not deceived by this convenient fiction. The inner world of human consciousness can also be found within, and not merely observed from without. We can listen to, and analyse, the movements of our imagination and of our desires, provided that we are not too frightened by that which we dimly suspect we may find there.

> My train of thought is the fruit of my reflections, is connected with my existence, my make-up. I am not able to change it, and I would not if I could. This train of thought which you blame is the sole consolation that my life contains.

If we are to be honest in appeal to Nature, as a value, we must start with that which we can directly know, and argue from the individual case to the general, and not, comfortably, in the opposite direction only. If that fond abstraction, Nature, has any design at all, its fine structure must first be legible in our own impulses and imaginings, when, fully analysed and distinguished, they are candidly set free in action and in words.

In its historical setting the force of Sade's solitary experiment in self-knowledge is obvious. He at least was neither surprised nor disappointed that the Revolution, when it came, was both liberation and terror. It had to have this double face. Therefore he could never share the illusions either of the moderates or of the Jacobins. But one may still find his voluminous works largely unreadable, because over-emphatic, thesis-ridden, unselected, and weighed down by the author's single-minded enthusiasm for his own discoveries. He is one of those still valuable writers whom it is easier to read about than to read.

Such casual brutality and disgusting privilege as his sadism, methodically practised, required seem inseparable from the peculiar conditions of living within an aristocracy just before its downfall. In Sade himself, inquisitiveness and self-analysis were an aristocratic passion, like gambling, which he was free, by virtue of his rank, to follow to its furthest limits. There is something of the amateur of genius also in his thought, of the self-taught inventor with a single obsession. But the discoveries are there, and the story of his life of absolute licence is now more fully documented.

6

The Theatre of Sade

THERE can be no doubt that Peter Weiss's play *The Persecution and Assassination of Marat as Performed by the Inmates of the Asylum of Charenton under the Direction of the Marquis de Sade* provided a theatrical experience of a high order: at least this is true of the play as it was performed by the Royal Shakespeare Company, directed by Peter Brook. It gave pleasure and it was interesting. The question is: Why and what is interesting about it?

It is possible to love the theatre and to revel in theatricality, to find the pretence and unreality of the stage wholly absorbing in its own right. It must be supposed that most actors and directors, if left to their own tastes and impulses, would strive after theatrical effects before all else. The satisfaction of any broader human interest might be quite secondary in their performances. But they are not left to follow their own addiction; they need an audience, and they cannot assume that every member of their audience will be as interested in the purely theatrical experience as they are. A mere playgoer will be interested in something that exists principally outside the theatre: in social change or political power, or in certain moral conflicts, or perhaps in poetry. A satisfactory play therefore, which will continue to attract an audience and by this means keep men of the theatre busy inside the theatre, must pander to one or more of these outside interests. So, obviously, Shakespeare and Molière did; but not so the Marquis de Sade, the

63

complete man of the theatre, consumed with theatricality, who all his life had difficulty in finding audiences to share, and to provide an occasion for, his endlessly planned theatrical effects. But at last, in the asylum at Charenton, he had a captive audience. He had also a cast that was ideal for his theatrical purposes, since their grip upon un-represented reality was likely to be as loose as his own. Sade could never tell the difference between lust and the play-acting of lust, between cruelty and the play-acting of cruelty, between being free and the play-acting of an ideal freedom. So completely was he a man of the theatre that he needed an audience before even the most elementary of his desires or emotions was real to him. All the world was for him a theatre, not only in the sense that he required a script and an audience for everything that he did, but also because he knew no distinction between acting and acting out, and between acting because he felt a certain emotion and acting as if he felt a certain emotion. Although he was an apostle of Nature in the eighteenth-century sense, his life was a theatrical artifice, its incidents a series of set scenes and illustrative tableaux. Every sexual experience had to be a complete drama in itself; that is why he needed odd combinations, carefully presented in his text for the occasion. The dictates of Nature could not be evaded; but they could be dramatized and expressed, with the only freedom possible, in play. To him the injunction 'Be natural' meant 'Dramatize Nature'. It has been difficult for his biographers to make his wife, mistresses, mother-in-law, the prostitutes and others, seem real to us, more than the trappings of one of his own dramas; his interminable writings, his stories and plays, are like stage directions for his life, and they outweigh the text itself.

It is therefore altogether appropriate that Sade, a largely unreadable writer and a man who had little or no influence on his contemporaries, should now be a household name and an emblematic figure. He was the precursor of show business, of the private life publicly acted. He was, in his life and his teaching, and, above all, in the relation be-tween them, the philosopher of theatrical curiosity, the man whose life was intended as a play, and whose actual plays were dead from the moment that they were con-ceived. His actions were commentaries, without intended practical effect, and his sexual exploits were histrionics. His life, both inside and outside prison, was a kind of phenomenological reduction, in which all the normal consequences of action were 'bracketed', placed in inverted commas.

Peter Weiss's original idea was therefore one of extra-ordinary brilliance: to make Sade the centre, and the commentator, of a play within a play, which would illustrate the full range of theatrical effects which the modern stage, after Büchner, Pirandello, Brecht, and Genet, can now provide. The material of the outer play is solid historical fact: Sade at last realizing his theatrical ambitions in the asylum at Charenton. There are two main intertwining, purely theatrical themes that connect our modern theatre with Sade's: first, the Revolution, or revolution, and the strategy of the élite of birth, race, and educated speech in the face of the inarticulate mob; secondly, the possibility of sexual licence, and the strategy of the ego in the face of the inarticulate instincts. For Sade, the proper strategy, whether within the body politic or within the individual, is to put on a show, to invite the high-minded, progressive audience, and to have fine

speeches made, about war and poverty and freedom, and
to wait for the audience to applaud noble, subversive
sentiments, which, in New York, it duly did. Thereby the
conflicts, simultaneously public and private, are tamed,
sublimated, purged, acted out, rendered fictitious, and
they become vicarious satisfaction for the perpetual
audience, bland and smiling on its raised seats, always
ready to peer in at any lively representation of lust or
suffering. Three elegant figures, seated at the side of the
stage, the Governor, his wife and daughter, bestow their
smiling patronage on the licensed antics and outrages of
the psychotic inmates. This is what we officially call Art
and Theatre. The performance, being art, must of course
be beautiful, if it is to earn aristocratic, discriminating
applause, and if the audience is to be moved: moved, that
is, not to action, nor indeed in any particular direction,
but just moved. Peter Brook's stage was consistently
beautiful, both in colour and in grouping; it was a constantly changing tableau, which subdued the violent,
obscene, unco-ordinated movements of the asylum's inmates to an aesthetically satisfying pattern, reminiscent of
Géricault. The stage was treated like a canvas which is at
all times kept lively and coherent. Even the indication
of semen on the trousers of the erotomaniac, Duperret,
can be seen as decorative, and the utmost horrors of
alienation and abjectness were subtly stylized. The musical
accompaniment, although appropriately strange and dis-
cordant, was also very pleasing, and contributed to the
aesthetic unity. The flogging of Sade by Charlotte Corday
is stylized, conveying a filtered erotic excitement to the
audience. Mr. Brook had arranged that the lines be
delivered in a careful stage diction, inexpressively, thus

underlining the extreme theatricality of the performance
within a performance. Sade has a languid, aristocratic
lisp; he plays with his English vowels and coolly experiments with words, listening to himself, amused by his
own rhetoric. He recounts the unspeakable tortures to
which the assassin, Damiens, was subjected, in detail,
quietly and slowly, in the reflective spirit of Jaques telling
the ages of man. He has known long ago that this is the
nature of man; man is a torturer rather than a killer, the
over-strained beast, with a nervous itch, an incurable
irritability, that is always generated anew in the cells of
his body. This he chooses to call morality. All punishment
is torture, whether it is the work of the courts or of the
citizen's guillotine. Sade cannot moralize and Peter Brook
and Patrick Magee, who played Sade, carefully indicated,
in style of performance, that he is now a self-absorbed and
curious commentator, not a revolutionary nor a reformer.

His sexual cruelty was an exacerbated curiosity, a child-
like desire to see the springs of the mechanism working
beneath the skin. Sade was a physiological determinist and
accepted the normal implications of this philosophy: that
all plans for moral improvement, or for the liberation of
men, are self-deception. Weiss respects this fact, and has
written a Lucretian speech for him. Love and war and
social domination, and the fantasies that accompany them,
issue from the imperatives of the body, the haphazard
concatenation of the cells, and can have no solution on a
political plane. Politics itself is an illusion, at best play-
acting, a theatre for the display of a given temperament.
Only a chemist could calculate the exact intervals that
divide the same from the insane, the feverish and ascetic
reformer from the erotomaniac and the sadist. We are

temporary configurations in the mad whirl of atoms, and our pretended civilization is only fear of Nature. The only real contact between persons is the sexual act, which is itself always a kind of rape, 'the contact of two skins and the exchange of two fantasies'. From Chamfort to Sade the step is from wit and worldliness to a grimly consistent metaphysics; Sade had seen the revolution fail.

Marat, Sade's foil, the paranoiac reformer with the irritable skin, is seated in his bath throughout the play, waiting for the predetermined climax—for the famous picture to come true, for Charlotte Corday's *coup de théâtre*. He rants, staring straight ahead with unseeing, already dead eyes, solitary and impotent, a man of words who makes no human contact, lapped in the illusion of free-will which still cannot soothe him. He has desperately to refuse to understand his own pathology, to keep talking, projecting in the form of a political programme his irritability and sexual deprivations. He must believe that the naked, natural man might be free, if he once throws off the trappings of his history; he is for a moment symbolically naked on the stage. But this hope, Sade implies, is a metaphysical mistake: freedom is not a historical and social category and cannot be a historical and social achievement. We can be free only if we suspend the reality principle and the control of the ego; a free man is at home only in the madhouse and, best of all, acting out his private fantasies on a madhouse stage. In the only gesture of normal communication on stage, Sade lays his hand on Marat's shoulder in sympathy; the social revolution is inevitably about to fail, to die, killed by its own children; but it was at least an illusion of freedom. At the postponed climax, when Charlotte Corday goes through the predetermined motions of stabbing Marat in his bath, the whole cast sighs voluptuously. The insane are now free in the ultimate disorder to attack the aristocratic and sane spectators; Sade smiles with satisfaction. The play-acting has done its work of liberation and is complete. It remains only for the cast of the outer play, as a sign of alienation, to reject the patronage of the audience in the real theatre with applause that ironically answers their benevolent appreciation.

It was a subtly contrived, superbly self-confident performance, almost faultlessly acted, continuously alive and interesting in many details that I have not mentioned: a theatrical success, a demonstration that a stage director can now again rival both cinema and opera in density of suggestion. Yet, as a play, *Marat-Sade* is in some ways deadening and depressing, or at least may be found so by someone who comes to the theatre for something other than the delight of theatre. This is because the play itself, beneath the glittering production, is cagey, allusive, and mannered in its treatment of its political themes. The central weakness, I think, is a lack of conviction and clarity in the writing of Marat's part. Mr. Weiss seems to be uncertain what a real and formidable political radicalism would now be. Facing Sade, who had descended from the superstructure of politics and society to the nether-world, Marat becomes merely a figure of superficial pathos and of the past, defeated and dead before he begins. And this is plainly not what the author intended or the argument requires. The old conflicts and arguments of the Thirties in Europe, between the liberty of the individual to follow his private madness and the needs of disciplined social revolution, are toyed with in a retrospective, civilized, detached way. Marat is, in most of his speeches, tinsel, stage scenery, or an element in a great painting. Again, the Brechtian songs are touching, but ironically and allusively touching; Charlotte Corday, the mad, beautiful country girl mouthing her lines, is again an element in a picture, an aesthetic contrivance. If one comes to the theatre with a coarse appetite, and not as an aesthete, one expects to be disturbed by a represented conflict, or by poetry, as by *Danton's Death* or *Rosmersholm* or even *The Blacks*. Even in Pirandello the theme of theatricality and play-acting is explored as a problem of Italian life and with a sharp, sombre realism. *Marat-Sade* is, in this production, an aesthetic delight and an apt historical pageant; but it is static, and the audience will leave the theatre without being assaulted or disturbed, comfortably appreciating the delicacies of theatrical technique. That, in a kind of bluff and double-bluff, this very theme is written into the play does not finally alter the impression. Weiss-Brook's *Marat-Sade* was a glowing spectacle and a luxury.

7

Letters of Oscar Wilde

O NE thousand and ninety-eight of Wilde's letters are collected in Mr. Hart-Davis's authoritative edition.[1] The letters form a design that is almost a commanding work of art, as Wilde would himself have wished. Almost, but not quite; because in the middle, disturbing the symmetry of the plot, is lodged the finally, definitely definitive version of *De Profundis*, superseding Mr. Vyvyan Holland's version of 1949. And the tone of this letter notoriously makes it scarcely a letter at all. It stands out. Wilde seemed to be filing a work of literature with posterity, for the record; and posterity, in its restrained and judicial way, has not been pleased. Invited to a kind of moral banquet, with no expense of style spared, as if to a spiritual equivalent of ortolans and champagne at the Savoy Grill, it has looked severely in the opposite direction, back to *The Importance of Being Earnest*, disregarding this expensive lapse of taste. Yet its inclusion is evidently right. Here restored to its context, the too calculated style of this letter to Douglas is more easily understood, and is less offensive, because it no longer seems as false as it seemed in isolation.

For Wilde at that moment, in prison, it was a condition of sanity that he should assume the attitude of one who reclaims his past by grandly understanding it. This was indeed an assumed attitude, a necessary pose, and the

[1] Hart-Davis, 1962.

71

quality of the writing often betrays it. But there is a psychological truth, fully recognized by the author, in this need for a theatrical success, for an exhibition of fine self-consciousness. He needed at that moment to hear the imaginary applause of a public temporarily silent, disloyal and departed. As Wilde remarked in another letter, the terror of prison was for him the vagary of emotion without action. *De Profundis* was action, a gesture. At no time in his life could he bear to be alone, because he must instantly translate overflowing feeling into extravagant performance, as physical energy must be expressed in movement. Posterity is a prig, and will always demand a terminal report on the measurable quality of the work done, abstracted from its conditions. But posterity may at last read the letter in its proper place, and judge, since judge it must, less harshly. As an oration at that stage of a drama which the public had chosen to recognize as public, the letter has force, aptness, and, in some passages, a quick psychological insight.

The real question, raised again by these letters, is the nature of the interest that we still take in Wilde, the ground of his claim to some kind of greatness and still rewarding originality. There is the obvious suspicion that this interest has little to do with achieved literature and its values, but is rather the romanticized prurience that attaches itself to the ruined rebel and to the vulgarly interpreted artistic personality: as to Gauguin, Dylan Thomas and others who, apart from their achievements, represent also commonplace dreams of scandal and of escape. Wilde himself knew that this part was open to him, and he later intermittently played it, summoning inept comparisons with Byron. But there is an evident interest elsewhere. He invented, without forethought, a style, a lightness and a verbal gaiety, which have passed in and out of English speech and writing ever since: it was as much an invention as Lear's nonsense had been, but less powerful, and wholly unpoetical, a gross trick with the English language, and it depends upon swift interruptions and an audience.

Gaiety, as a literary quality, is after all very rare; as with Sydney Smith, so with Wilde, it has been the achievement of casual and careless talkers, who would not hoard and concentrate their effects. The forming of the style can be watched in these letters. In Wilde it developed, and developed gradually, from enormous vitality, from the desire to please, from affectionate nonsense between friends, from the love of syntax and of the hard form of a sentence: certainly not from intellectual care or from any depth of reflection. It is not surprising to find in the early letters, among arrangements for shooting and riding with friends, that he placed *Aurora Leigh* alongside *Hamlet* and *In Memoriam*. He did not earnestly care for literature. It was only the idea of classical Greece, and of Flaubert, that engaged him, and never the less simple realities. Compared with the young Shaw, who was carefully to husband his physical energies, he begins and remains a free-spending amateur of letters, with massive, careless energy and with no stiffening of thin intellectual purpose. The opposing temperaments of these two Irish invaders, the one coarse and ample, the other thin and refined, are very exactly reflected in their style of wit, when their essays or letters or plays are placed side by side.

Wilde at his best achieved genial, liberating nonsense. He wrote proudly from Kansas City, during his American tour, that the miners, with whom he had been drinking, described him as 'a bully boy with no glass eye'. They were nearer the core, as disclosed in his letters, than the *Punch* cartoonists or Hichens in *The Green Carnation*. His aestheticism was a broad dramatization of a single idea—issuing from a huge enjoyment of the stage—and of the repeatable joke of mixing the conventions and artifices of comedy with ordinary social behaviour. He did not think about aesthetics closely, not even about the aesthetics of acting. He played variations on one theme: that of substituting the superficial for the profound, visible forms for spiritual states, as the proper objects of emotion; and this without any satirical intent. There was no moral and no meaning, and no one was ever threatened, except those who, in Yeats's phrase, were 'full of the secret spite of dullness'.

The letters startlingly confirm Yeats' famous account of Wilde's genius in *Autobiographies*, the most convincing that there is. 'He seemed to live', wrote Yeats, 'in the enjoyment of his own spontaneity.' Wilde himself claimed that 'joie de vivre'—his equivalent of 'enjoyment of spontaneity'—was, with will-power, the sole basis of art. Certainly this is the source of his dialogue in the plays, and reappears occasionally in the essays and in the letters—a wonderful euphoria, an extravagance of pose and pretence, which is an instant pleasure, instantly shared; it blows away reflection, and the prolonged anxieties of Ruskin and of Arnold which are its background. Something is 'as extinct as the dado'; Frank Harris is upstairs thinking about Shakespeare 'at the top of his voice'. These are echoes of the most remarkable voice since Johnson.

They are echoes only; Wilde was a talker, and not a

great letter-writer. He remarked that many men had been ruined, when they arrived in London, by the habit of answering letters: by 'ruined' he meant, of course, that they lost 'the enjoyment of spontaneity'. The quality of his gifts has to be read through these letters rather than in them. The letters are not in themselves of the sustained quality of Fitzgerald's, even less of Byron's or Lawrence's. But they tell the story of the years during and following imprisonment more vividly than it has ever been told before. On the other hand, the years of 'the parvenu' (Yeats again) when, a new Dick Whittington, he arrived in London, reluctantly leaving Magdalen, with his First in Honour Mods and Greats, and his ordinary under-graduate friendships, are not well represented. Oxford was a prelude, a period of innocent, easy charm. He had acquired a superficial classical manner, the gift of perfectly constructed sentences; and he carried away a false, scented, dreamy version of Greek culture, which he was later indolently to play with, as an anglicized, heartier Pierre Louys, a clubman among the asphodels, the friend of Mahaffy.

But there was not a hint of seriousness about his early successes. The seriousness of success began when the pavements of London did turn into gold. 'Success', he wrote untruthfully in a letter, 'is a science: if you have the conditions, you get the result.' On the contrary, for him it was a gift: there was no research. Yeats, insisting that he was essentially a man of action, compared him with Disraeli. He needed 'the contact of events', and for him this contact was Society. Unlike Disraeli, he never needed, and never had, patience and contrivance. The desire to please, and the superfluity of energy, were enough, whether in talk or overflowing in print. Odd episodes and uncertainties are recalled in the early letters: for instance, he earnestly solicited Curzon for an appointment as one of Her Majesty's Inspectors of Schools. But the letters become a continuous record of a speaking voice only during and after imprisonment, when friends were absent, and he was, after all the noise, alone.

The trial and the circumstances of imprisonment are detestable, and it is pointless to dwell on them, now that Labouchère's barbarous amendment no longer has its consequences in misery. Wilde's own accounting in these letters is clear. His 'heart', and his 'joie de vivre', were fully destroyed, and he became 'simply a self-conscious nerve in pain'. Of course he did not altogether change, and sometimes gaiety returned. As he realized, 'the world is angry because their punishment has had no effect'; he had no right not to be reformed. His motives remained, in their simplicity, the same after suffering as before, although he at first tried to persuade himself that they would change. The only difference was that he was poor, and cantankerous with his friends. That he was not guilty of some of the legal offences with which he was charged seemed to him irrelevant, and he was irritated by apologies made on his behalf: 'a patriot put in prison for loving his country loves his country, and a poet put in prison for loving boys loves boys'. He desperately tried and tested his friends, as letter after letter of accusation shows. The habits of friendship were the only morality that he knew.

This trial was severe. It is amazing that the friendships held – with Ross, Turner, More Adey, Ada Leverson, Adela Schuster and others. He apologized for his exactions – it was the only serious apology – in the terminology of a later probation officer: 'I was a problem for which there was no solution'. After his release he helped his prison friends, and his letters to the press about conditions in prison are rational arguments for reform, brilliantly expressed. But he found that he had no real purposes after release, because, true to his reading of Pater and to his 'half-civilized blood', he had no constraining habits, least of all habits of writing, of 'sedentary toil'. Talking was not a habit: it was the expression of his being. 'Between me and life', he had written to Conan Doyle, 'there is a mist of words always.' The echoes of his conversation continue in his letters until the end –with Ross, Dowson, Frank Harris, Rothenstein, Gide and, above all, with Douglas, mean, deceptive and odious in every relation displayed in this book.

There is always posterity's temptation to sum up and to judge, to count the achievement and the waste, and this in defiance of Wilde's own principle of spontaneity. At least he invented a new pleasure, a new resource of language in dialogue, used by conscious and unconscious imitators ever since: 'the essence of good dialogue is interruption', he writes in a letter. The reckless, generous charm, and the 'half civilized' genius, can still be felt in his letters.

8

⧏⧐

Letters of Freud

'BIOGRAPHICAL truth is not to be had.' This was
Freud's belief, more than once expressed in his letters.[1]
But at least historical myths can be destroyed. Freud's
personality has become the centre of myth, and it is not
difficult to see why. His thought, and his science, are now
entering a second testing period, at least in the West and
outside the Communist world. The moral and political
significance of his claims will be continually assessed in the
coming years, outside the clinical environment. But it is
always difficult to wait, to suspend judgment, and to look
at the evidence impersonally. Therefore a commonplace,
easily understood picture of the man is formed and diffused: the picture of a nineteenth-century materialist, a
scientific optimist, claiming to have discovered a path to
general salvation, omniscient and all powerful. It is a false
picture; indeed in some respects it is the very reverse of the
truth, or of such fragments of the truth as we can now
see. The letters show this, as did Ernest Jones's biography.
There is a characteristic tone everywhere noticeable in
Freud's writing: whether in these letters or in his books
and his papers, a sombre tone of resignation, of disillusionment, of disappointment, even of a quiet bitterness, as of
a man early exiled from hope. 'In my youth I was never
young', he writes in one of his letters. It is as if he had from

[1] *Letters of Sigmund Freud 1873–1939.* Edited by Ernst Freud, and
translated by T. and J. Stern. Hogarth Press, 1961.

78

the beginning found his own life disappointing, inferior to the demands that he had first made upon it. In the arrangement of this book of letters, we pass from a long series of love letters to Martha Bernays before their marriage, during the years of Freud's struggle for professional and financial security, and of his work with Charcot, to the early discoveries with Breuer and then on to the triumphant *The Interpretation of Dreams* in 1900.

The very early letters show a rough, strong, unnaturally mature person, energetic and undeceived, hardened against prejudice, deeply, and sometimes bitterly, pre-occupied with money, home, security. From the very beginning he mocks ambition, even scientific ambition. Later he refuses to be elated by his own manifest successes, and he is often gruff and awkward in the face of his admirers. There is always something defensive about this mockery, and at the same time there is a genuine dis-illusionment. 'Among my worst qualities', he writes, 'is a certain indifference to the world', and he writes also of 'a certain crust of indifference'. One can sense this under-lying indifference in these letters, in a rough, cynic tone that is sometimes very like that of Flaubert's letters. The denial of any exaltation in living, and even in the processes of discovery, seems to have become more pronounced with the years. The feeling of the letters suggests the very opposite of the conventional picture of a confident, nine-teenth-century rationalist and materialist. His affinities are rather with the disabused and ironical Viennese writers of the end of the century: with Schnitzler and with Stefan Zweig, and in Germany with Thomas Mann. And if one thinks of philosophy at all when reading these letters, one thinks of Schopenhauer.

But Freud himself distrusted, and even despised, philosophy, and despised the impulse in men from which it apparently comes: the urgent desire for a synthesis, for some single key that will unlock all the doors to natural knowledge, or for some formula that will make men feel at home in the world. He distrusted monistic thinking, all-embracing theories. They will only be the expression of the author's psychic needs, disguised as objective truth: and to him therefore repellent and weak, because of this disguise. The advance of knowledge calls, not for synthesis, but for analytical thinking, for the breaking-down of phenomena into their parts, for a minute attention to detail. 'Metaphysics', he writes, 'is a survival from the period of the religious *Weltanschauung*.' And the force of the word 'religious' here is that a metaphysical synthesis is consoling–softly consoling, but a consoling illusion. We cannot comfortably live with our own acknowledged ignorance, in an undisguised, untamed, untidy, unsystematized universe.

Towards the end of his life, as reflected in these letters, Freud would often be approached with suggestions for psychological answers to the world's problems, for some hopeful panacea that would transform human nature; indeed the suggestions, in their vagueness and generality, remind one of the popular neo-Freudians today. But Freud's replies are bleak and discouraging, and even contemptuous. Certainly he never at any time thought of his new science as providing answers to all humanity's ills, at least in its present state or in any clearly foreseeable future. Nor did he think that the form of this new science of the mind had been finally determined: He writes: 'Of one thing I am absolutely certain: there are certain things we cannot know now.' And again: 'I have surely not discovered more than a small fragment of truth . . . perhaps the psychology of the future will explain the workings of the mind by chemical processes: meanwhile, we must be content with what we have – the evidence of analysis.'

Throughout these letters one sees his need to check enthusiasm, premature optimism, that rushing forward of the mind towards omnipotent solutions. He writes in a letter to Groddeck in 1917:

Why do you plunge . . . into mysticism, cancel the difference between psychological and physical phenomena, and commit yourself to philosophical themes that are not called for? Let us grant to nature her infinite variety which rises from the inanimate to the organically animated, from the just physically alive to the spiritual. No doubt the Unconscious is the right mediator between the physical and mental. . . . But just because we have recognized this at last, is that any reason for refusing to see anything else? I am afraid that you are a philosopher as well and have the monistic tendency to disparage all the beautiful differences of nature in favour of tempting unity. But does this help to eliminate the differences?

'The infinite variety' and 'the beautiful differences of nature' – these phrases are not the phrases of a simple scientific optimist. Again of himself he writes:

I so rarely feel the need for synthesis. The unity of this world seems to me something self-understood, something unworthy of emphasis. What interests me is the separation and breaking-up of what would otherwise flow together into a primeval pulp.

He hated this pulp–anything that was soft, that is not ordered, divided, and hardly tested knowledge.

In a letter written towards the end of his life, Freud remarks that his achievement was more an achievement of character than of intellect. There is a sense in which this is certainly true, and in which it is true of most great and prolific writers and originators, when one carefully examines their lives. There has to be the drawing inwards of energy, the ruthlessness towards individuals, the persistence through suffering, and the acceptance of loneliness in work. Do any of the sources of this character appear in these letters? There are, I think, some partial suggestions. First, Freud's conception of himself as a father and leader, as a man of power, indeed as the figure of Moses. In this connection there is a most revealing early letter to Martha Bernays on John Stuart Mill and the subjection of women. He writes:

> It seems a completely unrealistic notion to send women into the struggle for existence in the same way as men. Am I to think of my delicate, sweet girl as a competitor? . . . I will make every effort to get her out of the competitive role into the quiet undisturbed activity of my home.

The note of masculine dominance and mastery here is characteristic; certainly it occurs in many places. The theme of the unalterable ancient father, noticed in Ernest Jones's biography, recurs at different points–for instance, in a moving letter to Max Eitingon in 1922:

So I suggest that we continue our relationship, which has developed from friendship to sonship, until the end of my days. Since you were the first to come to the lonely man, you may as well stay with him to the last.

He had to think of himself as the solitary leader, the Moses who might be left by his followers, and of course he understood this necessity in himself:

I am compelled to go my own way, often a round-about way, and I cannot make any use of ideas that are suggested to me when I am not ready for them.

His long path of advance was marked by desertions, as they seemed, the desertions of Breuer, Adler, Jung, Stekel, Rank. . . . Yet, in a memorable phrase, he writes of psycho-analysis as 'an exquisitely social enterprise'. And so it was in its heroic days, and so it still must be.

Freud did not conceal from himself his prejudices and the limits of his sympathy: for instance, his prejudice against American civilization and his attachment to Europe, his unalterably bourgeois tastes and habits. He knew that his observations were confined to the middle class at a particular time and place, and, in an interesting letter, he remarks that working-class culture may be significantly different. Above all, in relation to the Jews and to Zionism, he expresses himself in these letters with confidence and clear-sightedness, and with that rough self-sufficiency which seems to have protected him from anxiety, and, no less important, from waste of time. Fame, and the Nazi persecution of the Jews, brought new demands upon him, which he met. Up to that time, he appears in his letters as tranquilly at ease in Jewish ways of thought, and acutely aware of their part in the origins of psycho-analysis. He was at ease in the Jewish-Viennese milieu. When he finally arrives in 1938 at 39 Elsworthy Road, London, N.W.3, he is relieved to find, after the first shock of strangeness, that Primrose Hill is after all 'like Grinzing'.

One of the central mysteries in his life, to which one searches in vain for an answer in these letters, is an arithmetical one: his use of time. The mystery is in fact deepened, because the editor tells us that his father answered all letters immediately. How could he conceivably have found time to maintain his practice, on which his family's livelihood depended, and also to write the continuous stream of fundamental papers, case-histories and books, which seem to constitute a whole life-work in themselves? This problem ought to be a simple one, of dividing the available hours. But it is not really solved in Jones's biography, nor are there sufficient clues in these letters. So the fantastic story of the work prolonged until the end, with the long suffering from cancer of the jaw, is traced again here. The heroic vitality, the bitter contempt of success as of something that came too late to please, Freud's increasing pessimism about human affairs, are clear, sometimes too harshly clear. Some gentleness and naive impulse, missed in his childhood, were never recaptured. He writes:

> In the depths of my heart I cannot help being convinced that my dear fellow men, with a few exceptions, are worthless.

These chilling words must be remembered if we are to have a just, or even approximately honest, picture of

Freud's personality, and not only of his personality, but
also of his intellectual convictions. He was not a man of
the Enlightenment, who believed that human nature
could be radically improved. He remarks that 'the old
cultural levels are still alive, in the great masses'. And he
could still unshrinkingly use this phrase 'the masses'. The
horrors of the First World War were not, as is so often
said, altogether surprising to him–certainly not a refuta-
tion of his theory of human nature. He was less surprised
by them than Flaubert had been by the excesses of the
Commune, and less dismayed than Bertrand Russell was
by wartime emotions.

The more one considers his letters, and when one places
them alongside the evidence of Ernest Jones's biography,
the more clearly one sees a division in Freud's mind and
temperament; a division between his interests as a scientist
and his dreams of himself as an imaginative writer, almost,
one could say, as an artist. His strongest feelings, most
warmly expressed, are called forth by writers whom he
admired and who admired him: by Romain Rolland,
Thomas Mann, Arnold and Stefan Zweig, Schnitzler. He
is unduly pleased by their attentions, as he is unduly
indifferent to the attention of the rest of the world. He
tells Romain Rolland of 'the mysterious attraction' that
he feels towards him, and Schnitzler that he was 'his
double'.

Perhaps the most important single letter in Ernst
Freud's collection is a penetrating analysis of Dostoevsky,
as man and writer, addressed to Stefan Zweig. This letter,
and other casual literary criticism elsewhere–particularly
a few remarks on Don Quixote–show that 'double vision'
which is characteristic of the imaginative writer turned

critic. He holds apart his scientific understanding and his appreciation of imaginative depth, as so few of his imitators have; yet the one informs the other. The divided nature emerged in that wild enterprise of his old age, *Moses and Monotheism*, and in his obsession with Rome, with Michelangelo, and with Moses. Of course he shows himself aware of his unrealized ambition as an artist; indeed there is not the smallest trace in these letters of any naivety of action or response–except perhaps in that early letter about the competition of women and their proper place at home. This lack of innocence and spontaneity is perhaps part of the sadness, the harsh maturity, of these letters, as the years of great achievement pass.

The new ideas, which have transformed men's outlook and way of life in this century, have almost all come from the sciences. Philosophy, political theory, and even the literary experiments of this time, have been, by comparison, on the margin of intellectual advance. Freud, as he appears in his letters, was before all things certainly a scientist. But he was a scientist who also experimented on himself. The evidence of his self-analysis is altogether out of sight. But the personality that remains in view here is certainly not, and could not be, the whole biographical truth: the personality of a passionately self-willed man, secure and immovable in his home, disdainful and rather bitter, smoking endless cigars and counting Kipling's *Jungle Book* among his favourite reading, taking long walks in the mountains and dabbling in archaeology in his holidays, often wishing, as he grew older, to die and be at peace, and yet feeling his escape 'barred', as he wrote, by the survival of his mother. Those who read him, whether his letters or his scientific papers, for consolation or for reassurance, or for some brisk doctrine of adjustment to reality, will be disappointed. I shall end by quoting the words that he wrote on an occasion of death and loss: for the style here is the man:

> Although we know that after such a loss the acute state of mourning will subside, we also know we shall remain inconsolable and will never find a substitute. No matter what may fill the gap, even if it be filled completely, it nevertheless remains something else. And actually this is how it should be. It is the only way of perpetuating that love which we do not wish to relinquish.

9

Freud and Lou Andreas-Salomé

LOU ANDREAS-SALOMÉ was the intimate friend of Nietzsche and of Rilke, and a pupil, friend, and confidante of Freud. She was a sentimental tourist. She can be seen as one of the 'free spirits' of late romanticism, a voracious adorer, Ibsen's Rebecca West, a woman who urged men of intellect to assert their powers, and particularly their powers of intellectual destruction. Shaw, converting the heroines of Ibsen into figures of high comedy, would have been delighted by her. Her writings on the then fashionable topics of femininity and narcissism are often murky and tiresome, as romanticized biology is apt to be; they fall into a half-world of new thought, which is neither literature nor science. But the evidence of her *Freud Journal*[1] shows that the picture of her we have had so far has been incomplete.

There is an easy explanation of the interest that she aroused in such diverse men of genius: simply that she was an extraordinarily intelligent woman. She could grasp new ideas with a quite unfeigned clarity; she could immediately see connections which others could not yet see. She was therefore able to relieve the loneliness of men who had long taken it for granted that they would always be misunderstood, and therefore feared, even if the fear was masked by reverence. Freud was wholly at ease with her. She was quite free from the envy that any extrava-

[1] Translated by Stanley A. Leavy.

gance of imagination, or of intellectual power, arouses in most people. Her biographers, and biographers of Nietzsche, may speculate that her envy was of the other, the sexual kind. This cannot be known.

The Journal, written during her association with Freud in the years 1912–1913, when Lou Andreas-Salomé was fifty years old, shows a precocious understanding of his purposes and methods which naturally amazed him. He directed his lectures at her, solicited her comments afterwards, and was disappointed whenever she could not attend. Though the story of her relations with Nietzsche is well known, the story of Freud's lectures in Vienna, of the discussions of the disciples, walking home in the snow after the lectures, of the formation of groups and selection of favourites, of the crossing of the lines of loyalty involved in knowing Jung and Stekel – all this is not so well known. The atmosphere of the middle years of the founding of psychoanalysis in Vienna – something that is largely missing from Ernest Jones's biography, and even from Freud's published letters – is alive in this Journal.

Behind the gossip and anecdotes, often in themselves delightful, some of Freud's own uncertainties are revealed. One sees more clearly why his tentative speculation was so often converted into hard doctrine: why he found it necessary to be so absolute in insisting on his theoretical distinctions, even when the clinical evidence, still minute in quantity, evidently left many alternatives open. He was frightened of being welcomed as a philosopher. It has already been remarked that Freud both disliked and distrusted philosophy, or anything that resembled it. One reason for his distrust is more than once suggested in this book. Psychoanalysis could in those years, and in that city, very easily have become one more variety of new thought, an eclectic philosophy of life, or a key to a new *Weltanschauung*.

In the period of the *Last Days of Mankind*, as Kraus recorded them, or of the decline of the west as Lou Andreas-Salomé believed, new doctrines of regeneration were springing up all across Europe, as they had in the late Hellenistic Period and in other periods of anticipated disaster; and nowhere more feverishly than in the Vienna of Mahler, Schönberg, Wittgenstein, Schnitzler, and Kraus. In his association with Fliess, Freud had come close to the abyss that separates medical science from a regenerative philosophy of the soul. When the pull was constant towards a higher synthesis of philosophy and biology, towards a California-style doctrine of salvation, Freud had to over-compensate in the opposite direction, if psychoanalysis was to survive at all as a branch of clinical psychology. The over-precise mechanical metaphors, the doctrine of psychological forces, the pseudo-quantitative explanations of conflict, amounted to a kind of promissory note; this note might perhaps be redeemed later when a more adequate physiology was available. In the meantime, the appearance of scientific precision, even if it was sometimes illusory, might serve its purpose of keeping philosophers of the soul at bay.

As Lou Andreas-Salomé noted, this was part of the significance of the battle with Jung. The concept of libido, with its unique expression in sexuality, prevented psychology from being satisfied with explanations in purely mental terms. The danger that Freud saw in Jung's hypotheses, as in all the heresies which rejected his concept of sexuality, was that they suggested explanations in terms of the concept of the mind alone. They thereby cut the cord that might at some time re-unite clinical psychology with physiology. Freud contrasted philosophy with science, not only as seeking syntheses rather than a more minute analysis of the data, but also as explaining behaviour in terms of ideas only, whether conscious or unconscious ideas.

Although he mocked, he could tolerate Lou Andreas-Salomé's philosophizing, because from the beginning she understood his strategy of driving neo-Freudianism, as an eclectic doctrine of mental healing, outside the movement. She might wilfully speculate on the relation of mind and body, and on Freud's resemblance to Spinoza; but she agreed that sexual drives and feelings must be the centre of psychology, if only because they are already the accepted point of contact between the physical and the psychical realms. Freud himself always turned away from general speculation of the kind that engaged Lou Andreas-Salomé, just because her speculations could not suggest specific and testable solutions to specific problems. He sometimes can be seen to be wearily hoping that problems, when stated in his terms, would allow specific tests and solutions; in those early stages it was essential to keep up the appearance of tentative advance rather than to fall into the surrounding morass of philosophical generalities. In the last twenty years one has seen how empty, and how consoling, neo-Freudian generalities can be, particularly in sociology. Freud loathed consolation; for him the first condition of science was the suppression of wish and the postponement of total solutions.

There are pictures of Freud in Lou Andreas-Salomé's Journal that deserve to be remembered. 'He enters the class with the appearance of moving to the side. There is in this gesture a will to solitude, a concealment of himself within his own purposes.' One encounters again his wilful melancholy, his tired and persistent pessimism about human beings and their opportunities of happiness. It is as if he had abandoned all spontaneity in an earlier existence, and was now, in some attenuated form of life, looking back upon the unavoidable errors of normal experience. His disillusion seems to have been so radical as to cause him, after his marriage, to deny, like Spinoza's free man, that any mere passive emotions, unmodified by irony, could be imputed to him. He often speaks here as if he were only reflecting on experience, which for him was in the past and complete, as a man in mourning might speak. Ten hours of analysis during the day would be followed by the delivery, or preparation, of lectures in the evening. His living was working; and only in his emotional demands upon his followers does his temperament appear in this Journal. The reader of the Journal must, therefore, be warned of frustrations: upon introducing Rilke to Freud, Lou Andreas-Salomé writes: 'I was delighted to bring Rainer to Freud, they liked each other, and we stayed together that evening until late at night.' That is all. The Journal is both fragmentary and egotistical in this way.

Coming to psychoanalysis from literature and philosophy, Lou Andreas-Salomé did not seriously question its scientific credentials: in this she was typical of her time. Vienna in 1912 was the decaying centre of Europe in which the beginnings of the new music, of the new architecture, of the new philosophy, the new psychology, were being sketched and formed, as parts of a general revolution of ideas. We cannot now deny that the revolutionary ideas of this century have been mainly scientific ideas–in physics, biology, and in the mathematics of probability, logic and information theory. But in a longer perspective this might turn out not to be the whole truth. For the dividing line between the empirical sciences, as previously defined, and other human inquiries may now be less clearly marked; those inquiries which lie on the margin of science may still prove surprisingly fruitful. Freud's hypotheses, judged by existing criteria, were at many points improbable guesses, elaborated in the terminology of an exact science. In the process of analysis itself, he had invented a variant of scientific observation; for the fantasies that he detected in free association and in dreams were to be detected through interpretation. And interpretation was a procedure of literary and aesthetic inquiry and of literary and aesthetic explanation. In his own life, as he is partially revealed in reminiscences of him and in his letters, he alternated between two poles: at one extreme was the requirement that he should be a pure scientist, and that his theory of repression and of neurosis should be precise, and should be spelled out as a scientific hypothesis; at the other extreme there was the requirement that he should be a kind of artist, who needed extraordinary sensitiveness, and a suspension of disbelief, in uncovering the fantasies concealed in most forms of human expression and behaviour. The hybrid that results is unintelligible without the same aesthetic and scientific culture which he inherited and preserved. An empiricist philosopher will be repelled by a hybrid claim to knowledge, which substitutes interpretation for mere observation of the data as its base. How can there be theory worthy of respect which does not rest

on unchallengeable fact, independent of interpretive insight? This principle of exclusion, as applied to claims to
systematic knowledge, may be unanswerable. But at least
a similar hybridness can be suspected in other tentative
inquiries which are characteristic of our time. For example,
he who studies as scientifically as he can, the forms of
language and the process by which a child learns language,
might find that he cannot isolate the unchallengeable
phenomena which his theories are required to cover. The
isolation of distinct phenomena in this field may not be
independent of interpretations, which in turn are to some
degree guided by the theory. If this were the situation,
and if therefore theories of language were less than scientific judged by established standards, it would not follow
that the inquiry was uninformative and useless. It would
follow only that alternative reconstructions were possible,
and that certainty had not been achieved. One cannot
always know in advance whether a given complex subject
matter–e.g., the forms of language or the content of
dreams–is susceptible to a scheme of explanation that has
proved adequate in the natural sciences. The material that
is of interest may be just too complex, and we may
need to be satisfied, at least for a time, with a hybrid
understanding of it.

In these early years Freud was not in a position even to
guess what limitations upon precise knowledge he would
encounter. He could only go ahead, and Lou Andreas
Salomé's Journal shows at least some of his strategies:
above all, his two-sided attachment to an idea of himself
as an empirical scientist and also as an imaginative interpreter of the language of the passions. The interpretations
are made to fit the theory, and the theory is adjusted to fit

the interpretations. The argument is therefore circular, and we have no detachable conclusion, which so far constitutes systematic knowledge. We are left with a method of inquiry, indefinitely extendable, which shows the mechanism of repression at work, and which may always be used to retrieve some of the ideas and wishes that are repressed, and to recover some of the energies that are lost.

IO

◄◄ ▶▶

Henry James

L EON EDEL's life of Henry James,[1] is, in its method
and scope, in its discretions and also in its naivetés,
typical of this time. As one reads, one follows a long-
drawn-out match, a patient game of skill, played between
the living biographer and his dead, but not defenceless,
subject. It is still too early, with the fourth and fifth
volumes still to come, to decide whether the defence will
prove stronger than the attack.

For Professor Edel, as for most of his contemporaries,
the sources of the imagination are no longer to be
accounted a mystery. On the contrary they pose a problem which may be solved by a sufficient accumulation of
psychological clues. There is, and there must be, a central
secret, a figure to be discerned in the deceptively woven
carpet of James's personality. By a kind of biographical
cryptanalysis, the figure may finally be thrown into relief,
the unifying secret may come out. For the assumption is
that any considerable writer has involuntarily encoded his
inner nature in his art; then posterity, in interpreting him, is
challenged to recover the key; it will be found in the least
edited documents, in the least calculated utterances, of the
subject. And so contemporary biography requires minute
research, and a readiness to pounce on every betraying
detail and every significant coincidence.

There can be few more exciting subjects for this con-

[1] *Henry James: the Middle Years*, 1884–1894. Hart-Davis, 1963.

temporary style of biography than Henry James; indeed
Professor Edel's pursuit of the missing clues might well be
the theme of a James story of the middle years, and en-
genders the same suspense. For James, like Stendahl, it
foresaw posterity's attack and, unlike Stendhal, prepared
his defences against it. He kept a careful watch on all
documentary evidence which might inconveniently survive. He emitted a copious, all-enveloping smoke-screen
of social trivialities which would conceal much of the
target from the pursuers, whether of his own time or later.
He cultivated a massive indirectness of language in his own
autobiographies, as in his fiction. He contributed to the
legend of the aesthete, the mandarin of art, the remote
master, who scarcely touched the crude realities below
the surface of social comedy. This legend, or much of it,
lasted until the 1930s, when, with the James revival, it
gradually collapsed. It was too evidently in conflict with
the substance of the novels and with their felt relevance at
that time.

James returned again and again to the theme of the
defence of 'the private life' against prying eyes, the penetration of secrets as a form of power, and even as a form of
erotic excitement. *The Sacred Fount* was the climax of this
obsession. Perhaps we shall have a better understanding
of this late, strange, repellent work when Professor Edel
has finished. The succession of confidants, first-person
narrators who are pure observers, the watching women,
are active agents in his novels and stories in virtue of their
cruel determination to know, of their worrying their way
into a view of forbidden relationships. As James presents
them, following the laws of his own imagination, the
proving of secrets has all the intensity and excitement of a

love affair or of a campaign; there are pitched battles of dialogue, feints and encircling movements, glorious victories when the last outworks of decent dissembling fall before predatory minds.

His narrators and confidants feed on the victims of their curiosity, secure in the corrupt power which their worldly knowledge brings them. The innocent are those who do not yet know, or who will never know, that there is always a secret evil, some perversity of power or passion, below the bland surface of any adult and civilized way of life. The great fortunes, the worldly ease and the spectacle, the precarious decencies of Edwardian London and of Anglo-American society, concealed perverse contrivances and immoralities. The penetration of these secrets, and the counting of the cost, was not only the main theme of his novels, but the motive power of his imagination, connecting his fiction with his intimate experience. Writing to Gosse after Walter Pater's death, he confesses that he envied the way in which Pater had concealed himself behind his work; Pater had achieved 'the mask without the face', while he still had to protect himself from 'exposures, accidents, disasters'. He is still protected, but only just.

The only exposure, accident, and disaster in the third volume is James's cautious, uncertain relation with the American lady novelist Constance Fenimore Woolson, who finally threw herself to her death from a window in Venice. Professor Edel makes it plain that we cannot know precisely what part James had played in their long, intimate association in Florence and elsewhere, nor whether the suicide was closely connected with James. The most dramatic episode of the middle years shows James abandoning his theatrical ambitions in London for ten days to join Miss Woolson's sister in Venice after the suicide. If there were letters and other documents, he must be in a position to dispose of them; and he was.

This intrusion of violence is a diversion, a disaster indeed, but without a sequel. Year by year James's confidence and self-sufficiency, his command of his environment, as of his art, become more and more firm. The long-prepared strategy, of society and solitude duly balanced, is beginning to succeed. The suicide of Miss Woolson, and the failure to make money by writing plays, are the only reverses in his middle years.

It is again clear that James's philosophy was always closer to that of Balzac and Zola than to Flaubert and Pater. He had nothing in common with 'the babyish decadents' of the Nineties, or with any French doctrine of art for art's sake. Vitality, and the exuberance of creativeness, were the qualities that he himself possessed and that he admired in others. Some of the stories of the middle period have passages that are vulgar, novelettish, facile; at their worst, they are fluently written, smart magazine pieces. In several of them, the author is too evidently pleased with his own virtuosity, beaming and shining with the sense of his brilliance and worldly understanding. But the gross energy, the copiousness, never fail; and when he feels himself ready for a subject with a broad sweep, as in *The Bostonians* and *The Princess Casamassima*, the literary high spirits, the superb flow, carried him forward. There were no Flaubertian groans, or fears of sterility. James was not an exquisite, contrived, fastidious writer. Following his progress in these pages is like reading about the foundation of a great American manufacturing fortune:

there is the same ruthless planning and egoism, the same pride in output. He was a professional, rather than a priest, of art. He despised amateurs. Professor Edel shows him attending relentlessly to contracts, conditions of publication, lengths, and editors were reminded that he was determined to earn his own living.

When James talked about form in fiction, as he so often did, he was talking about the story-teller's concentration of interest, exactness of timing, management of scene and dialogue. Form was not a surface beauty, a purely aesthetic quality, as (in different ways) it might be in Flaubert or Anatole France. It may be argued that all art is the exact calculation of intervals, and that its essence is an inspired placing or timing. But in one aesthetic (that of the aesthete) the paradigm of form is typically found in a Chinese vase; in another in the skills of a light comedian, who by subtleties of timing can make inert material live, and seem expressive of an abundant, surrounding life. James's idea of form brought him nearer to the second aesthetic than to the first. He wished to hold and to dominate his public, and he suffered deeply when he failed on the stage, and when his sales remained low. The purpose of fiction is to bring a more intense awareness of the moral contrasts, and moral possibilities, too loosely presented in the social scene. Like Strether in *The Ambassadors*, he invoked Life, when called upon to justify his own 'doings'; and he liked to think of writing as his form of action. To William James he wrote that he was unable to do much reading, since 'I produce a great deal': 'the great thing is to be *saturated* with something – that is, in one way or another, with life: and I chose the form of my saturation'. It is a mistake, he insists, to another correspondent, to 'found oneself on so many rigidities and rules–so many siftings and sortings'. Appetite and abundance was his principle, and not fineness and good taste.

He needed in London–the London of *The Princess Casamassima* and of a famous essay–the daily visible evidences of strong energies, the monuments to greed and rapacity in great houses, and the evidence also of their unavoidable cost in squalor and misery: he saw 'the under side, the wrong side, of the London world . . . the strange, pale, mouldy paupers who blinked and stumbled in the Piccadilly sunshine'. As a conscientious realist, he grimly visited Millbank prison, which he described as 'a worse act of violence than any it was erected to punish'.

In *The Aspern Papers* there is the passage in which the narrator looks up at the equestrian statue of Colleoni, 'the terrible condottiere . . . on the high pedestal on which Venetian gratitude maintains him'. This is the pure Jamesian version, perfectly expressed in *The Golden Bowl*. Cruel energy and civilized achievement are inseparable: ruthless egoism succeeds and time gives it the patina of respectability and of culture. These are the world's values and James, like his narrator, did not dispute them. In the social worlds of London, Florence, Venice, and Paris, he moves like a great predator fish in his element, taking what he wants as he passes and then proceeding on his way alone. He will have his monument, and no scruple or weakness will divert him.

I still have a suspicion that the artist's defence may indeed prove stronger than the biographer's attack, that the secrets of 'the private life' will not be known, and that the whole face behind the big, bland mask will not be exposed.

II

◄◄ ►►

William James

IN 1890 both *Principles of Psychology* and *The Tragic Muse* were published. William James remarked to Henry that the year 'will be known as the great epochal year in American literature'. He was not deceived. The two brothers had stepped outside the provincial setting into which they were born. They had both known that it was their mission to establish a full and distinct American presence in modern thought and literature. They had both felt constrained and diminished in that small, far-away corner of the world, Cambridge, where 'life is about as lively as in the inner sepulchre'. Each was to make his escape, with some difficulties and slowly, from an excessive spiritual refinement and to affirm his independence; but they had different strategies. That William finally stayed and Henry went; that William made himself a national figure, was proud of native resources, and found a philosophy that looked peculiarly American, while Henry found his models in European masters and in European manners: these are the familiar facts. Now that we have Professor Allen's biography alongside Professor Edel's volumes on Henry, both based on family sources, the story can be seen to be very complex.

A preliminary apology may be needed for thinking of William James in this Shem and Shaun setting as part of a brotherhood and a family and not simply as an original philosopher standing by himself. There is a personal reason, a bias. From the early 1930s onward Henry James's novels and stories, and the concealed character that they half reveal, have been of almost obsessional interest to many Englishmen. When in 1934 a friend took me to see Jacques-Émile Blanche, the then aged portrait painter, who had known most of the great writers and painters of his time, both in England and in France, he was surprised and irritated that two undergraduates should come from Oxford to ask him about Henry James. Everything about the family seemed then, and still seems, relevant.

The reason for this curiosity is not obscure. Henry James was the first and most authoritative witness to be heard on 'the international problem': that is, on the elusive differences between American and European experience and manners, and on the typical dislocations that occur at any point of close contact. The history of the James family and of their European journeys, and Henry's stories and novels, together illustrate the first phase of the return of Americans to Europe to test and to measure themselves, and to find the true nature of their difference and of their uniqueness, in Europe. He was at once a modern artist and a modern prophet. The James family, with their second-generation wealth and educated confidence, were highly articulate harbingers of the future, which turned into our present.

The letters and journals quoted in Professor Allen's biography add the detail of journeys, and reflections on journeys, which are missing from Henry James's *Notes of a Son and Brother*. While William hesitated between science and philosophy, Henry's whole future as a go-between and interpreter was determined in these early family visits to Europe. He was to become more far-seeing, and less deceived, about the deeper differences between European and American attitudes than any writer before or since. Anyone who has been placed at a point of contact between American and European ambitions, and has felt the surface tensions and tried to understand the dynamics of them, can still find no better textbook from which to start than *The Golden Bowl*. The harsh realities of the balance of power, and of the balance of innocence and corruption, taking different forms on the two sides, are there summed up with an unequalled prescience. Henry James saw both sides, because he was divided, and was mocked by his brother for being so divided.

William had little contact with the world of Mr. Verver, with the new American fortunes, with the hard little men who came to Europe to buy treasure, bringing that narrow, sharp caution and control of impulse which would wear down their pleasure-loving adversaries. The contrast between the brothers, which fills their letters, was very far from simple. As Henry's genteel circumlocutions concealed immense energies and a concern with the mechanisms of society, and with the power of possession and of property, and concealed also an iron will to succeed, so William's frank and breezy style concealed the most sensitive perceptions, metaphysical doubts, and self-doubts. William descended to depths of brooding despondency and of loss of normal impulse which were unknown to Henry, who was finally less fastidious, less gentle, and less vulnerable, and more sure of his vocation.

As a young man William could write to a friend, 'All last winter . . . I was on the continual verge of suicide'. He suffered from a succession of nervous illnesses and a continuing hypochondria. James came to think of philosophy itself as a form of hypochondria, a diseased pre-occupation with the possibility of finding a stable value in existence. Toward the end of his life, he was to say, 'Healthy animality, what would I give to have been educated in it'. For him the existential problem had always been the relation of the mind to the body, the relation of thought and the will to the mechanical and chemical causes which physiologists study. He had two ideas of the self and of personal identity, both of which were irresistibly vivid to him, and which he could not put together without anxiety and a sense of conflict. His own efforts of will in overcoming his nervous weakness and moods of disgust were an undeniable reality, a datum of experience as primitive as anything to be observed in a laboratory. But the spiritual powers which seemed to govern his inner life could neither be plausibly identified with, nor disconnnected from, the causal connections that a mature psychology would discover. Characteristically, he could allow his emotions to be identified with the per-ceptible dispositions and behaviour that revealed them. But the inner core of personality, the struggling self that would contain and direct these passions, ought to be 'something solid within my breast'.

He could often, and particularly in his later years, see himself, with his metaphysical anxieties and efforts of will, as being a representative case for clinical study. But he would turn around and, like his father, claim 'the right to have a say about the deepest reasons of the universe'; and this seemed to presuppose some independent and superior vantage point within his mind. If the solid centre within his breast was felt to give way and to melt into the sea of natural phenomena, ebbing and flowing according to its own unalterable laws, he would feel himself disintegrated and insane. This in fact happened in the crisis which is tentatively placed in the spring of 1870, when he was twenty-eight. This breakdown is probably described in a well-known passage of *Varieties of Religious Experience* as the experience of an unnamed Frenchman. He had looked into 'that pit of insecurity beneath the surface of life', and it was a revelation of an emptiness and powerlessness, of a missing mainspring. The anxiety lasted for some months, and could be described as 'a horrible fear of my own existence'.

It is one aspect of the genius of James, and of his modernity, that to inquire into the psychological origins of his philosophy is not to imply even the smallest disrespect. He anticipated the inquiry himself. In a sense he was the first truly modern philosopher, because he hoped to understand the mechanisms by which philosophers, not excluding himself, project their inner conflicts and anxieties upon the universe, and because he was for this reason incapable of the pomposities which philosophers ordinarily use to protect themselves. He knew that his symptoms of conflict had often been the occasion of religious conversions: how natural that, in the emancipated James household, they should prompt an obsession with the freedom of the will and with the problems of personal identity and dual personality. He could not press his self-analysis very far, if only because he had not even the outlines of a tested theory with which to work. His phenomenology of philosophical attitudes was largely guesswork and literary intuition.

Professor Allen's biography, like *Notes of a Son and Brother*, brings out the indecisiveness, the ineffectiveness,

[1] William James' by G. W. Allen. Viking Press, 1967.

the enveloping spirituality, the damaged and amorphous personality of his father, together with his great nobility of mind, 'in the stiff, stupid house' of James's childhood, as a severe witness described it; the sons, and some outside observers, thought of it as a house held together by women. The manly ideal that James set himself required that philosophy should take one into the open air and toward the frontiers of scientific exploration, and that the effort of discovery should be in the same mould as mountain-climbing in the Adirondacks. His lectures and teaching at Harvard imparted this manliness and strenuousness in discovery, which naturally appealed more to Gertrude Stein, his pupil, than to his colleague Santayana, who noticed principally 'a pathetic sincerity'.

James turned away from the ineffective ruminations, the beautiful consolations which seemed to have separated tender philosophy from the positive sciences. Of Josiah Royce he remarked: 'The subject is not really vital to him: it is just fancy work'. Royce is here made to represent the typical academic philosopher, with a fine edifice of theory to his credit, assured, admired, and intellectually bland: the serious philosopher. James never became, in this pejorative sense, a serious philosopher, and he was always fretting and restless within an academic setting. He had no time for 'the cool, dry, thin-edged men who now abound', a typical phrase which reveals his distrust of those who 'made a business of philosophy'. He recognized the uncomfortable genius of Peirce, the greatest of American philosophers, and did what he could to help him. His greatness as a teacher was to inspire independent inquiry and he lent a new dignity to his profession in America.

As a philosopher he was original in having converted a very specific demand, which traditionally had been the starting point of metaphysics, into a demand laid upon psychology. He had to find 'some stable reality to lean upon' which would remain constant in the flow of his experience; this was his 'strongest craving', but it was to be satisfied only within a setting of strict naturalism. His conscience would not allow him an appeal to some special form of knowledge, or access to reality, unknown to the sciences, which is the ordinary path taken by those who, like Maine de Biran, had craved for some guarantee of a stable self.

The Principles of Psychology is a masterpiece which remains entirely readable because of this tension and connecting theme, and because of the directness, absence of pretence, almost naïveté, with which he exposes his difficulties. The Augustinian search for the centre of mental activity is pursued in a light, experimental, entirely modern tone, which is almost the tone of conversation. The book was also brilliantly organized, and its chapters fixed distinct topics of inquiry for some generations ahead. It carries the weight of dead psychological and physiological theory, and survives. Like *Portrait of a Lady*, which contains some similar reflections on personal identity, its language is unforced and easy and is enjoyed even by those who dislike Jamesian bravura. *Varieties of Religious Experience* of 1902 is rather a more superficial work, looking back to the cultivated opinion of the last century rather than forward to the philosophical concerns of our own time, to George Eliot rather than to the contemporary philosophy of mind. In the later years, after 1902, James had 'a feverish, personal ambition' to achieve a philosophical synthesis. He failed. Lacking a hard logical structure, his later philosophy may be valued as suggestive and lively essay writing.

The story of William James's life is in part the story of intricate relationships within the James family, and of his efforts to overcome depressions, vacillations, and his psychosomatic illnesses. His immense charm, his shrewdness, wit, impatience, and integrity can be felt in his letters, and James emerges as an irresistibly amiable and serious man. His comments on popular lecturing recall *The Bostonians.* He found himself 'meeting minds so earnest and helpless that it takes them half an hour to get from one idea to its immediately next neighbour' and then 'they lie down on it . . . like a cow on a door-mat, so that you can get neither in nor out with them'. He felt like saying to his eager audiences, 'Smooth out your voices if you want to be saved'. The note of aristocratic impatience here was common to the family, who must have felt themselves to be a first family of the mind, centrally placed in Cambridge, facing toward Europe and away from the great uncouth settlements further West, where Mr. Verver was making his millions and getting ready to buy beautiful things and beautiful thoughts.

The word 'experience' was for both William and Henry, sons of an enveloping genteel house, a sacred word: as if, in pursuit of that which they would each count as experience, they were invalids finding their way out of a dim sick-room into the sun, from a banal and settled virtue toward the discovery of uncertainty and of coarser appetites and open possibilities. It is sometimes thought strange that William James could spend a lifetime thinking about the relation between mind and body and about the emotions, without inquiring into the nature of sexuality, which intuitively might seem to be the central case of this relation. He was contemporary only with the beginnings of this inquiry, and he was at least open-minded about Freud's suggestions and he was in touch with experiments in psychological medicine. He remained until his death open to any new range of experience, believing, in his brother's words, that 'experience is never limited, and it is never complete'; value resides in the process rather than in the product. He said finally of philosophy exactly what his brother would say of the art of fiction, 'there are no fortunes to be told, and there is no advice to be given'. If fortunes are to be told, and advice given, this must be the work of his earlier profession: experimental psychology, which is a branch of medicine. For much of his life he had felt himself to be near to the boundary that divides sanity from the disintegration of the self; and he had kept himself away from abysses of depression with constant effort, with the felt pressure of a will for sanity, and for a normal engagement with the external world. Science was for him a symbol of health and metaphysics a relapse: so there is a moving directness, and urgency of personal need, in even his most theoretical writing.

12

◄◄ ►►

The Autobiography of Bertrand Russell–I

FOR many decades Lord Russell has been disclosing his more intimate feelings, and his views on private and public morality, to an enormous public. During his long life his emotions, his changing opinions, and many of his experiences in love and in friendship, no less than his face and the sound of his voice, have become a familiar part of the public scene. Alongside the history of his development as the original master of the modern movement in British and American philosophy, there is another history of the popular moralist. In a steady flow of books, articles, and famous B.B.C. broadcasts, he has shown himself to be extremely gifted in addressing a very large public in a style that is at once elevated, direct, and easy.

When he gave the first set of Reith Lectures to be broadcast by the B.B.C. not long after the war, a vast audience listened; and many people, who would not count themselves as belonging to an educated minority, stated that they would feel his death, when it came, as a personal loss. He was felt to be the exemplary intellectual of his time, at least in England, and his existence was felt to be an encouragement, just because his intellect did not seem to have isolated him from common concerns. Like Bernard Shaw, whom he despised, he had been an unsubdued guerrilla force operating on the margins of organized opinion, and outside all institutions, living in the open; but, unlike Shaw, he had never asked for a licence as a comedian of the intellect; he remained a philosopher, without compromise.

Yet one has always had the impression that his facility in self-revelation, and his willingness to live on the public stage and to advertise his public purposes, still left much of his own inner nature untouched and separate. Partly because the self-exploration was so unnaturally fluent, lucid, and continuous, it seemed that it could not be complete, and that it must be, at least in part, defensive. The truth about his own motives and impulses could hardly be as tidy as he was suggesting in those unfailingly pointed, gay, and resilient sentences.

The first volume of his autobiography gives substance to this doubt. Alongside the familiar, always articulate, exemplary, endlessly self-explained, masterful Russell, another Russell appears, scarcely less original and no less interesting, but less accessible, implied rather than declared. This other Russell is a pessimist, always in flight from 'the bane of solitude', and, like other pessimists, he takes refuge in prophecy, and is inarticulate in the description, or in the expression, of emotion and of emotional relationships. He has made a legend of his childhood, and the sources of his memory, and therefore of imagination, have become dry and too much used. A mood of melancholy runs through this history of magnificent achievement.

This first volume can be read as a sequel to the *Amberley Papers*, which was the first description of Russell's origins and childhood. One has a long sweep of intellectual and social history, unsurpassed elsewhere in English literature. Russell, the second son of Lord Amberley and Kate Stanley, was dandled on the knee of his grandfather, Lord John Russell, who had been Prime Minister, and who remembered the beginnings of the century and had been near the centre of the ruling aristocracy throughout Victoria's reign. Bertrand Russell was surrounded by rumours of great affairs, and was brought up under the influence of a grandmother and an aunt, amid a cloud of masterful or eccentric uncles and cousins. He recalls the alliances and marriages linking aristocratic families, perpetually visiting each other. He was intensely solitary, introspective, and almost an orphan in the great houses of his childhood. He therefore became, and remained throughout his life, a natural diarist and autobiographer, making the world, and his own place in it, real to himself by finding phrases that would define for himself his own nature. He looked for the meaning of his life in arguments with himself; and this flow of argumentative monologue became part of the substance of all his later experience, underlying his experience of love and of friendship.

His mother and his sister died when he was two, and his father died a year and a half later. His 'people' had given their lives to causes, to social reform and advanced thinking. Proud of his inheritance of public responsibility and unconventional opinion, his awareness of his origins was predominantly intellectual. It seems that from his very early years men and women were differentiated for him principally by the propositions to which they subscribed. His efforts as an adolescent to formulate his own beliefs–about theism, free will, the nature of mathematical knowledge, and utilitarian ethics–were at the same time a necessary effort to create his own character. To the dismay of his family he was to emigrate into the remote middle classes by his marriage to an American, Alys Pearsall Smith. Yeats used to denounce the Russell family because, with their Whig opinions and advanced thinking, they had brought the depressing and unaesthetic ethical culture of the middle classes into the aristocracy. This marriage to an American Quaker was a further step in the direction taken by his father in his friendship with Mill and the Grotes. Repelled by the heartlessness and mindlessness of the true aristocracy, he had tried to assimilate himself to the prigs and the bourgeois.

At Cambridge Russell had emerged from his solitude into a society in which emotional relationships could be founded on common beliefs. The external world and his private world had come together. The letters and memories of this time have a wonderful ease and assurance, and one is relieved, as one reads, to come into the light after the gloomy splendours of Pembroke Lodge and of high Victorian society. With G. E. Moore, Whitehead, Keynes, George Trevelyan, and later, with Gilbert Murray, he immediately belonged to another peerage, the peerage of genius. These were all men who knew that they were born to intellectual power, and who knew that they would make great tracts of intellectual territory their own. Their letters and the remembered exchanges between them have a well-sustained stateliness, as if they were diplomatic exchanges between reigning houses of the mind. When Russell is on a walking tour in the West Country and stays alone in a country hotel, he seems in the letter he writes to be like Haroun-al-Raschid descended among ordinary men. While living in London, he disdains the scurryings and agitations of the crowds in the streets, who are, or seem to be, unconcerned with eternal truths. This was, but probably no longer is, an elevated Cambridge tone. It is not surprising that Russell's friend Wittgenstein, a Tolstoyan by conviction, was unwilling to become an apostle, that is, to be received into the secret Cambridge society, going back to Hallam and Tennyson, which constituted a body of the elect, bound together by mutual admiration, and renewed in each succeeding generation.

In spite of, or because of, this justified sense of superiority, no one has equalled Russell's power to address the scurrying man in the street on philosophical issues. Just because he had himself first turned to philosophy when he urgently needed a firm foundation of belief, a *Weltanschauung*, and a remedy for his emotional uncertainties and isolation, he has always had a point of contact with those who expect from philosophers, and from intellectuals generally, the old consolations of philosophy, and particularly a sense of purpose. These consolations academic philosophers are usually incompetent to supply. To Russell, as to Mill, Bradley, James, and Wittgenstein, it had always been inconceivable that one should think of philosophical problems without also thinking of a superior form of life, of a fundamental re-direction of interest which would answer to a need for perfection and remedy a deep-seated discontent. He has had no use for the discontinuities of consciousness, which are encouraged, or at least permitted, in academic thought no less than in academic painting and literature, and which give a pejorative sense to the word 'academic'. Like Hume, but for a much longer period, he had that sense of the emptiness of all human effort, and of the instability of all opinion, which is a natural source of philosophy. The surprising thing is that

this almost religious sense of the vanity of human achievement, and of the worthlessness of everything imperfect,
contingent, and perishable, persisted in spite of his discovery of his mission in mathematical logic, and of his
partial fulfilment of his mission. Some of the moving
story of his famous discoveries in logic, and of his periods
of defeat and discouragement, when he could not solve his
problems, is briefly told here.

The reader is given some faint idea of the concentration
of creative energy over many years which was involved
in the completion, with Whitehead, of *Principia Mathematica*. But the undertone of deep pessimism, of a metaphysical melancholy persists and is felt as a threat, and has
to be resisted before it is engulfing. A very similar mood
lies on the surface of Bradley's writing, which exploits a
fin-de-siècle satiety and despair, felt as a reaction against
the hopes that had been tied to material progress, and as a
reaction against the abstract optimism of utilitarian philosophies. That there was this far-from-obvious affinity
between Bradley and Russell beneath the strong intellectual opposition is shown in letters that Russell prints:
letters of mutual respect, as from men who had felt the
same discontent and strangeness in their time. The later
academic followers of Bradley and of Russell might
despise each other, as epigones will, and there were
philosophers at Oxford in the 1930s who, supposing themselves to be following Bradley, presumed to tell their pupils
that Russell was a logician with no deep understanding of
metaphysics. Liberated by Moore, Russell very soon
passed through his early Hegelian phase. But it is now
easier to see why he sometimes wished that he had been a
contemporary of Spinoza, and had been able, with a good

conscience, to construct a metaphysical system. In the early years of the century, and before the new positivism of the Vienna circle had been formulated, he had the suspicion that systematic philosophy might now be 'hopeless'. But his own intellectual temper was incurably philosophical and not at all scientific. He needed to find, or at least to look for, very general truths which he could certify by his own powers of argument, and which would give a rational structure to his emotions. It is worth remembering that Wittgenstein, who became Russell's pupil, had as a young man looked for the source of morality, not in a prohibition against murder, but rather in a prohibition against suicide. The disenchantment and lassitude, sometimes turning into disgust, which were so common among the more imaginative European writers in the decade before 1914, at the high tide of liberal and bourgeois culture, do not appear in Russell's public personality, and appear only fitfully in his writing. He overcame them; and his marvellous vitality carried him forward into public causes even before 1914, and even while he was refounding his study of logic. But he had felt an immediate sympathy with the shades of pessimism, and with the distrust of progress, in Conrad, Bradley, and Wittgenstein.

Much of the material of the first volume, which ends in 1914, has appeared in various forms elsewhere in Russell's many confessional writings. One central episode is new: the story of his first marriage. The story is harsh and rather chilling, because of the abstract prose in which it is recounted, as if a report or a judicial summary is being rendered; the lessons of experience are given, but the experience itself escapes. The empty space is filled by fine writing about ecstasy and love, rather in the manner of his essay 'A Free Man's Worship'. This fine writing seems to serve the same purpose as the conventional phrases that less gifted men use to divert strong feeling into harmless channels; it buries the past. Nothing is visualized, and one is left without detail and without the means of imagining the events. There is a curious mixture of willed frankness and of instinctive reticence in the narrative, which has a stoic nobility.

Russell seems often, as an autobiographer, to see his own life as a journey of moral exploration, a pilgrim's progress. So strong was his need to find an objective justification for his emotions that he seems to have been continuously writing his life while he was living it. So his autobiography has a startling clarity and an absolute honesty of one limited kind. But nowhere is there the smallest gleam of unconscious memory, and therefore of imagination, which enable the reader to feel the past as it was experienced, and to catch the quality of some experience of love or friendship or intellectual excitement. The remembered people, most of whom bear famous names, are briskly described and their views are characterized; but they have a two-dimensional reality only, like the members of some Cabinet thirty years ago. There is a sense in which he does not really remember his past at all; he has turned his emotional energies toward planning his future, and these plans include drawing lessons from the past. He has developed for this purpose a hard, glittering, and imposing style, which is like a beautiful screen, intensely enjoyable in itself.

As one comes, too soon, to the end of this volume, one realizes with wonder that three or four men's span of experience and activity are waiting to be included in the next volume. He has already written the lectures on German Social Democracy for the opening session of the London School of Economics, the first of his books and among the first adequate discussions of Marxism in English; but the classical investigation of Russian Bolshevism is in the future. He has already discovered the Theory of Descriptions, but logical atomism is still to come. He has already discussed our knowledge of the external world in the Lowell lectures at Harvard, dictated in one draft, as he reveals; but the bulk of his work in epistemology is still to come. He has still to go to prison, and to China; he has still to found an experimental school, to write books about marriage and happiness, which are a kind of moral fiction, related to moral philosophy as science fiction is related to science. The beginnings of all these interests are recorded here; and the eloquence of some of his letters in 1897 is scarcely distinguishable from the eloquence of statements that he has made in 1967. It is an ageless eloquence, a tone of voice that will never be forgotten.

13

<hr>

The Autobiography of
Bertrand Russell–II

As there are religious conversions, there must be philosophical conversions also. Since the eighteenth century, philosophy has taken over some part of the ground that once belonged to institutionalized theologies, as a focus of divided feelings. As soon as God is no longer well defined and can be either invented anew, or dismissed, in each generation, the relation of man as a species to the rest of Nature becomes open ground for philosophy. It is to be expected that natural protestants, who are also sceptics, and whose emotions follow their intellect–such men as Hume, Mill, James, Russell–will meet sudden crises of belief, moments of conversion, in which they see Nature as overwhelming them, or as supporting them, or as offering them reconciliation and rest.

Russell's Autobiography, no less than Mill's, is clearly constructed around such movements of conversion. It has the form of a pilgrim's story. The pilgrim progresses through various philosophical trials and uncertainties toward a final resting-place, from which, looking back, we can see his progress as emblematic. In successive episodes of disillusionment, he changes his way. He passes under the influence of men who have shared one or another of the conflicting attitudes to Nature which are present in his own mind, unreconciled. G. E. Moore, Whitehead,

Gilbert Murray, D. H. Lawrence, Wittgenstein, each had some rôle in a crisis of belief, which was at the same time a turning point in a continuous unfolding of unrealized emotions. Alys Russell, Ottoline Morrell, Constance Malleson, Dora Black, are each associated with a new phase of moral commitment or of moral exploration. Every attachment is given a defined meaning and a direction. The author's requirement that the phases of his life should all have a legible significance has its natural satisfaction in autobiography. The form allows a sign-posted story, with clearly marked transitions and conclusions, as in the best Whig histories.

Russell's original need to understand his place in Nature, and to render some definite account to himself of the value of his existence, has often amounted in its urgency to a kind of rage. His recurring disappointments, as he describes them, became moods of inner fury. If the world will not be as it ought to be, he will imperiously call for an immediate explanation, or he will rail upon it like Timon with an extraordinary energy of pessimism. And then, as the story is told, he is picked up once again, and enabled to continue on his path, by some other superior spirit, who equally cannot submit to the tawdry contingencies of a common fortune. Or he may meet on high ground, and with almost wordless understanding, another aristocrat who will neither bend nor break before the wretchedness and triviality of events: this happened to him with Conrad. The search can then proceed with some relief from loneliness and under a new encouragement.

There is no hint of autobiography as comedy, as in Sartre's *Les Mots*. The search is philosophical in the fully traditional sense: there must be a vantage point from

which the limits of rational freedom and of useful knowledge will appear necessary, or at least will be explainable
and acceptable. Until the vantage point is found, the choice
of a way of life must seem arbitrary and unstructured, and
this is intolerable. The ordinary flow of events, of marry-
ing, of having children, of making discoveries in mathematics and philosophy, by itself makes no perfect, or even
proper, pattern which will satisfy a philosophical temperament. If the play of normal instincts and of their derivatives
are to be considered self-justifying, then violence and
cruelty have also to be accepted as natural necessities.
Russell could never so accept them. He has tried to
believe that that which is horrible in the actual world is
mainly due to a bad system: 'tried to believe' only, because he also shares Conrad's 'sense of fatality', of the
incurable disjointedness of human nature and of his own
nature.

For Russell the great war, and the loyal responses to it
throughout Europe, had brought into total discredit the
moral systems on which European societies had been
based. Philosophy must fill the gap; a rational man must
work by himself, an enemy of the crowd, and re-invent
morality. In this respect, and particularly in his pejorative
use of words like 'the system', he anticipated, as early as
1916, many of the attitudes of radical students today. He
called upon moral imagination to undermine that bourgeois authority which requires loyalty in time of war,
character-forming discipline in schools, and the repression
of sexual variety. These three pillars of decent society are
still the targets for attack by the only genuine radicals that
we have. And of course Russell has always disdained and
rejected the rights of private property, not only in theory,

but also in his own practice. He gave his unearned wealth to others.

Russell is very conscious of nobility as a virtue, and of the proper rôle of a sage, who stands, like Spinoza, alone, near to nature in half-intellectual, half-mystical, understanding and therefore in opposition to society. Again he writes, 'Spinoza, always, is right in all these things'. His own nobility is most evident when he is least aware of it. In his second volume there is at least one truly noble episode: his visit to the Soviet Union in 1920. He was hoping that there he would at last find the necessary new, and socialist, society. He felt to the full that temptation to substitute faith for evidence which overwhelmed so many intellectuals after the war. Yet his descriptions of the Soviet Union are painfully truthful, and the seeds of evil in Lenin's system of government were seen at the very beginning: 'I wonder whether it is possible to build a body first, and then afterwards inject the requisite amount of soul. Perhaps, but I doubt it.' The report, sketched here, was made in full in *The Practice and Theory of Bolshevism*.

In this volume there are very few references to Russell's strictly philosophical discoveries in the years from 1914 onwards. Yet much of the work critically examined in D. F. Pears's important book *Bertrand Russell and the British Tradition in Philosophy* was published in those years. By 1914 Russell's principal contributions to logic, as opposed to the theory of knowledge, were already in the past. But he was at least an intermittent source of ideas in metaphysics and in the theory of knowledge until 1940. He had formed, and then had lost, two philosophical friendships which will always be recorded in the history of thought: first, the friendship with Whitehead, from which

Principia Mathematica had issued: secondly, the friendship with Wittgenstein, who was associated with the theory of meaning and of truth that was called logical atomism. Both friendships ended in rejection and discouragement. Russell publishes here a rather cold letter from Whitehead in January 1917 which denies Russell the opportunity of seeing Whitehead's new philosophical work before it was in final form; this letter marked the end of their collaboration.

Far worse for Russell had been the onslaught upon his philosophical abilities by his former pupil, Wittgenstein. In 1916 Russell wrote to Ottoline Morrell: 'His criticism . . . was an event of first-rate importance in my life, and affected everything I have done since. I saw he was right, and I saw that I could not hope ever again to do fundamental work in philosophy. My impulse was shattered, like a wave dashed to pieces against a breakwater. I became filled with despair.' He dryly notes that he soon recovered from the despair; but Wittgenstein had persuaded him 'that what wanted doing in logic was too difficult for me. So philosophy lost its hold on me. That was due to Wittgenstein more than to the war.' The criticism had given him 'a sense of failure', because he had always believed that 'fundamental work in philosophy' must be logic, in the sense that he had given to this disputed term: that is, an investigation of the possible logical forms, and therefore of the necessary clear syntax, of any propositions that could be assessed as either true or false. Once these concealed logical forms, the deep structure of literal thought, had been clearly distinguished, the traditional questions of metaphysics would, he believed, be exposed to precise answers. Wittgenstein had carried this Russellian programme forward to an extreme conclusion in his *Tractatus Logico-Philosophicus*: it was a conclusion that Russell could not accept, and could not even find wholly intelligible, although he had arranged for the publication of the book and had written the Introduction to it.

Russell was to continue the programme for many years, linking the theory of meaning with the theory of knowledge, while Wittgenstein turned along a quite different path. He decided that he and Russell had misconstrued the relation between the abstract structure, which logic, as the theory of mathematical truth, investigates, and the grammar of spoken languages. The theory of meaning must be started again from observation of language as it is. The complex grammar of a natural language cannot be either justified, or corrected, by reference to any deeper principles of sentence-construction which mathematical logic may suggest. The Russellian plan of sketching in outline the forms of a logically clear language, which is free from the vagaries of natural grammars, must misfire. The forms of natural grammar, carefully described and interpreted without philosophical prejudice, are all in order as they are. The apparent illogicalities and untidinesses of the forms of spoken languages serve their complex functions in making communication possible, much as the apparent illogicalities of social custom can, when properly interpreted, be seen to fulfil a function in holding societies together. A philosopher is in no better position to impose, in the name of rationality, a simplified syntax on natural languages than is a social anthropologist to impose simplified patterns of behaviour on the society that he studies. In both cases the first duty of the inquirer is to respect the complexity of the facts, with the belief that the complexity serves a purpose, and that it has a natural explanation. But for Russell, in all things a reformer, philosophy loses its sharp edge and purpose as an inquiry, if it is not a recasting of the customs and institutions of language for the sake of greater clarity and distinctness of statement.

Soon after the war, he was therefore alone as a philosopher, without collaborators; and one may even find a desultoriness and lack of full conviction in his later work in the theory of knowledge, which now looks more like a chaos of clear ideas than the confident working out of a programme. He had lost contact with later discoveries in the philosophy of mathematics, and he was altogether out of sympathy with the descriptive philosophies of language which Wittgenstein and others were developing.

The second volume is haphazardly put together from letters with scattered commentary and occasional shreds of narrative. The prodigious richness and variety of Russell's interests and achievements in these years – the life of four men – are implied rather than presented: the method is one of glimpses. Marriage to Dora Black, the visit to China, to a civilization in which, as an aristocrat and a rationalist, he was at home, and to Japan, where he could hear no echoes of the eighteenth century and where he was not at home; the birth of a son, and the revolution of feeling which this entailed; the foundation with Dora Russell of their famous free school; the finely written, money-earning books on morals and marriage and happiness and education, and the conquest of a large public; the primitive, ridiculous 'hue and cry' raised in America when, a notorious immoralist, he accepted academic appointments there. The episodes flash by, and the reader has to fill them in with his imagination.

There are incidental pleasures in the author's irony. For instance, a wonderfully typical letter from a Professor Hocking at Harvard about Harvard's difficulties is printed -typical that is, of the prudent and moderate academic mind's reaction whenever a hue and cry is raised, balancing pro and con with no sense of the absurd. Although Russell felt humiliation, or at least a poisoning sense of disgust, in America in the years just before and during the war, he knew that he had achieved much of his ambition, which, apart from philosophy and mathematics, was 'to change people's thoughts': 'power over people's minds is the main personal desire of my life'. After the discouragements from Whitehead and Wittgenstein, he had seen himself as 'starting on a new career. . . . I have something important to say on the philosophy of life and politics, something appropriate to the times'.

In fact Russell's 'philosophy of life', so often and clearly defined, has not been appropriate to the times, at least since the first war. He has not been involved in, or greatly affected by, new tendencies in philosophy, psychology, literature, or in political and historical thought, except when they complemented an intellectual attitude which he had already formed before 1920. His 'philosophy of life' has rather served as a reminder of better times, when starvation and physical suffering were admittedly even more widespread than they are now, but when genocide and the destructions of war were less terrible, and less high-minded in intention, than in this century. It is a repeated theme of his that 'the eighteenth and nineteenth centuries were a brief interlude in the normal savagery of man; now the world has reverted to its usual condition. For us, who imagined ourselves democrats, but were in

fact the pampered products of aristocracy, it is unpleasant':
or again 'for the next 1000 years people will look back to
the time before 1914 as they did in the Dark Ages to the
time before the Gauls sacked Rome'.

The poison of disgust is produced by that particular
mixture of vulgar, democratic, and dull self-righteousness
with mechanical barbarity which he, like the radical
students, finds in contemporary American policies: all
sides of his nature are offended equally. Judged by the
standards of the society that is described in *The Amberley
Papers*, the pseudo-species, pale-faced man, has been,
first steadily, and then precipitately, going downhill since
1914, in the sense that the horizon of expected improvement has contracted. It was possible to believe before 1914,
and perhaps for a few years after the first war, that this
pseudo-species was endowed with an adaptive intelligence
that was sufficient to find the fitting social forms for rein-
forcing the general stock of intelligence. J. S. Mill rested
his philosophy upon this belief, which he did not seriously
question. Russell was never a Comtean optimist by
temperament, and his doubts have grown stronger and
stronger over the years. From his very early years he had
reasons in his own experience for sharing Conrad's 'deep-
seated sense of fatality governing this man-inhabited
world'. This sense of fatality is 'the something else' which
he has always been half saying, even while he writes of
reform and improvement, and which permitted his intimate friendships with Conrad and with T. S. Eliot.

His is still an autobiography that celebrates an un-
bending confidence in self-determination and in the
efficacy of the conscious mind. There is no suggestion that
the purposes of rational men are commonly cross-purposes,

and of the compulsion to repeat patterns of behaviour; therefore a life can be seen as a progress and as a learning by experience, almost as if it were a scientific inquiry. That element in human behaviour that makes puppets plausible is nowhere represented: the limited repertory of expression and gesure in any individual, the disconnections and abrupt reversals in conduct, and the expected repetitions that compose a distinct character and that seem to leave no alternatives open. The confession of a static, absurdly contrived nature, which is delightful to some philosophers, such as Sartre, who are obsessed with the contingency of any individual's interests, is not permissible in Russell, for whom there must always be freely willed development, and true self-assertion.

14

Wittgenstein

'THE spirit of this book is a different one from that of the main stream of European and American civilisation, in which we all stand.' So Wittgenstein wrote in 1930, in the foreword to the series of short paragraphs and detached sentences that make up his posthumous *Philosophische Bemerkungen*.[1] As a philosopher in the tradition of Augustine and Plato, he was concerned to 'grasp the world not through its periphery – in its multiplicity and variety – but at its centre – in its essential being'. The former way of understanding is the way of the scientist and of the scholar. Their knowledge is cumulative, increasingly complex, dispersed, and technically refined. The spirit of their inquiry is the spirit of progress, and they are subject to the law of the increasing division of labour, to the need for methodical co-operation. At every stage of discovery, the world reveals new facets, demanding new ingenuities and a new vocabulary. The way of the philosopher towards understanding, according to Wittgenstein, is an opposed and complementary one. His is the way of solitary meditation on the deep structure and grammar of our most commonplace thinking. Wittgenstein always believed that there was an unmoving centre of doubt and incomprehension which no discovery, either in the sciences or in logic, could remove. Here, an ordered advance, the application of a common method of investigation akin

[1] Edited by Rush Rhees. Blackwell, 1964.

to scientific method, was an illusion, an illusion that had recurred in his time in the guise of a sure and teachable method of philosophical analysis.

Wittgenstein was writing this book in the aftermath of the Vienna Circle's proposals for the future of philosophy. Their new philosophy was to be a disciplined, rational reconstruction of the concepts of science and of a logically clear language. For the mature Wittgenstein this could only be a diversion, a movement away from the centre of difficulty towards the surface and periphery. In philosophy we do not need theories, and more precise methods of analysis; on the contrary, we need to forget theories, and to look at the most simple facts of common speech, which have been hidden beneath the accumulation of past philosophies. As elsewhere in his later writing, the imposing discoveries of contemporary logic and mathematics are referred to only as examples of a way of thought that may suggest, but can never solve, a true philosophical doubt, which is also a doubt about the most ordinary and familiar points of contact between language and the world. If we can see even the beginnings of a highway to disciplined solutions, we have moved away from pure philosophy, which will always remain a wilderness, a desert landscape with scattered, and more or less solitary, figures.

A philosopher, if he is more than a functionary of culture, has withdrawn from the ongoing business in the intellectual market-place of his time; he is in retreat in a self-made desert, dedicated to his own mission of examining the bare rudiments of our knowledge of the world. His motives have to be of a certain purity. He must want to stay away from the intellectual market-place in which useful and complex ideas are freely exchanged. He concentrates, without compromise, upon unproductive questions. He knows that he will by his own choice be intellectually lost, that he may seem foolish and ineffective, and that he will invite general hostility, because his withdrawal from the normal rush of positive discovery will be seen as subversive and threatening. He will learn less from the finished writings of his contemporaries than from an intense exploration of his own doubts and confusions.

This conception of philosophy as an otherworldly calling, a renunciation of the comforts of intellectual progress, is plainly a modern version of an old tradition. The true philosopher is an initiate who recognizes other initiates, and he can be distinguished from the journeymen clerks and professors who carry on the regular business of the schools. It is appropriate to this tradition that Wittgenstein should want to say of this book that it is written to honour God, but also to say that this would be misunderstood. A philosophic piety and respect, a respect for fact, in the face of that which is finally incomprehensible in our situation, has a religious character. At least, he explains, his book should be written from no motives of vanity and should be in this respect pure. There is, of course, no doctrine of a perennial philosophy here, no orthodoxy or transcendental assertion. The spirit of retreat and of dedication has survived without the now dead letter of theology. The perspicuousness (*Durchsichtigkeit*) at which a genuine philosopher aims, in trying to see through to the skeleton, the bare bones, of the conceptual scheme, is of a peculiar, kind: his insights are not verified and are never conclusive, and they cannot be usefully detached from the probings in which they are embedded. One cannot carry away the conclusions, detached from their supporting arguments, and apply them outside philosophy. They will be significant only to those who have felt in their own experience the same sense of mystery. They are a recognition of the strangeness of what is obvious and familiar in our claims to knowledge.

Wittgenstein's own life was in fact given up to a continuous philosophical meditation, and anyone can now see, in these notebooks, how concentrated his thought was, how purely philosophical and undistracted by any outside interest. He was in this sense a Spinozist and not a Leibnizian: this opposition of two philosophical temperaments has its contemporary counterparts. Two ideas of seriousness are at issue. The first, Wittgenstein's, is the idea that serious philosophy is autonomous, a self-governing domain, to be kept pure and uncontaminated by tourists, who do not share its peculiar rational obsessions and for this reason can carry nothing essential away. The second, Leibnizian idea of seriousness in philosophy, very much alive now, is an opposite one: philosophical inquiries are effective, and therefore serious, in so far as they become a not exactly distinguishable part of the general advance of systematic knowledge in modern logic, mathematics, psychology, and linguistics. There is no essence of philosophy, or of anything else, and only librarians and university administrators need to be concerned with divisions of subject-matter, which are ultimately arbitrary and uninteresting. There is no virtue in perplexity and wonderment, in keeping alive ancient and imprecise problems for which no exact method of solution has yet been suggested. If we free ourselves from this mystery-mongering, from the solemn and prophetic tone and the pretensions of the elect, which are inherited from the ages of faith, we may be able to break down the old problems into more tractable elements, and then to look for gradual, methodical solutions. What is now needed is co-operative and detailed work, technical invention, and not solitary meditations, which make a virtue of their inconclusiveness.

The late J. L. Austin in England, and Professors Carnap and Quine in America, have in their different ways worked to change the tone of philosophy and to moderate its pretensions to uniqueness; they have required their followers to work prosaically for specific and usable solutions, employing common methods of inquiry, regardless of whether their results are to be labelled 'philosophical' in a sense that Plato and Augustine would have recognized. Their pupils are not to be withdrawn from the main stream of inquiry in their time; they are to work with the new scientific grammarians and linguists, with mathematicians, and even with the theorists of machine technology, turning away from ivory tower and monastery.

Both schools of thought, representing at once different temperaments and different ideals of clarity, contribute, through their opposition, to the vitality of contemporary discussion. And they have a meeting-place, or disputed ground, in the differing accounts that they will give of the alleged distinction between statements that are necessarily true, and of which a denial is unthinkable, and statements that are only contingently, and as a matter of experience, true. Wittgenstein relies at many points in this book on the distinction between that which is unthinkable and that which is merely false. His concern is to explain the limits of the thinkable.

In the years 1929 and 1930, when this book was being

prepared, Wittgenstein was still freeing himself from the bonds of a theory of knowledge and of language which was originally Russell's. The peculiar logic of descriptions of sensations and of the look of things: the nature of infinity; the application of mathematical truth to the world; the logical barriers to knowledge of the mind of another person; the structure of space and of time reflected in grammar–these are some of the main topics. One sees again how closely packed, how undeviatingly relevant, his thought was, and how graphic, and immediately responsive to his own needs, his style of writing; the free form, without the conventions of exposition, did the work of a philosophical dialogue, and is a less artificial form. Visual metaphors, natural to a designer and architect, and an understanding of the explanatory power of models and of visualized schemata, make his thought always accessible and vivid, never altogether abstract. And a sense of the importance of the inquiry, of its centrality as a human concern, comes through, even when the immediate topic is described as the grammar of colour words. Wittgenstein, having taken Augustine as his model, evidently found philosophical confessions his natural form of expression. Sharply aware of a future public, he still needed to make no concession, to adopt no public and conciliatory manner, and he could follow only the connections that were significant to him, in a continual search, which was the way of life that he had chosen.

15

◄◄►►

Doctor Zhivago

THIS essay was written during the week of the publication of the English translation of *Doctor Zhivago* in
1958. It is inextricably attached to the events, and to the
feelings, surrounding the publication. I have therefore left
the contemporary references unaltered, including the
references to Pasternak as a living person. The essay may
recall the event in its contemporary setting.

That *Doctor Zhivago* is one of the great novels of the
last fifty years, and one of the most important works of
literature that has appeared since the war, seems to me
certain, even when every allowance has been made for
the circumstances of its appearance and the effect that this
may have upon one's judgment.

The immediate enthusiasm with which it has been
received is not in the least surprising and is no ground for
suspicion. This enthusiasm is, I think, quite unconnected
with politics in the narrow sense and with Communism,
or with any sentimental sympathy with the author's
frustrations. The explanation is that, at first reading, a
Western European is immediately reminded of all that is
best in his own past, of the great tradition of full statement,
which he had come to think no contemporary writer
could now resume, because the extremes of violence and
social change had made any real imaginative reconstruction
of the recent past, any whole picture, seem impossible.

We have come to take it for granted that the most serious art of our time must be fragmented art and indirect statement. There has for a long time seemed no possibility that anyone should have survived who, in the exercise of his genius, retained all the literary ambitions and philosophical culture of the last century. That it has happened is an extraordinary accident. It is as if, in the general devastation, one lane of communication with the past has been kept clear and open. Perhaps only a long isolation in a cultural desert could have produced this result, this slow maturing of a work that is independent of any distracting contemporary influences. The fact remains that part of the immediate excitement of the Western reader is a sense of escape and of nostalgia, of a return to the real or imaginary Golden Age, when absolute assurance and uncontrived and confident gestures were still possible.

Doctor Zhivago is unlikely to have any great influence on the writing of novels in France, Britain, or America: it is too far away from the main stream and it has been too little affected by the experiments of the last thirty years. It really does seem to come from a lost culture, to be just coeval perhaps with Thomas Mann's *Buddenbrooks*, but certainly not with Faulkner and Sartre. This free, naïve, as opposed to sentimental, writing is probably not something that can be imitated or further developed, because the confidence in a complete philosophy, tested by revolution and violence, of which the naïveté is an expression, is probably everywhere lacking in the West. Pasternak is after all looking back in this novel, and leaving his testimony, proved by his experience and final. Since his experience includes the Communist revolution, the looking back is not mere looking back. He has come to terms in his own mind with that way of life which has the most plausible and widely advertised claim to represent a future. In contrast with this, most writers in the West are in an uncertain, waiting condition, becalmed in a recognized interregnum, not knowing the worst and therefore incapable of any tested, unqualified statement. It is not surprising, therefore, that they turn to naïve or sentimental mannerism, to expressions either of despair or of uncertainty. The whole sum of shared experience in forty years of violence cannot be yet calculated.

The difficulty that this novel presents, after a first reading, is the difficulty that any carefully composed and long meditated work of art presents. It is naïve art, in Schiller's special sense of the word, but far from naïve, in the ordinary sense, in its composition. The English translation, as English, is certainly better than we are used to in translation from Russian, although the familiar jolts of incongruity do sometimes occur. It allows one to guess that the vocabulary of the original is rich and elaborate, particularly in descriptions of nature and in the dialogues of the poor. But not knowing the original is evidently an enormous loss, which cannot be mitigated. The whole book is informed by an intense feeling for everything that is distinctively Russian, by a characteristic kind of mystical patriotism, which is quite unlike the patriotism of the French or the English; the feeling of Russian landscape and Russian talk are evidently conveyed exactly in nuances of diction that will have deep associations for any Russian. The endless talk and the endless landscape are as much part of the substance of the novel as the revolution itself, as being the constantly changing background of the central story of love and separation. The vastness of the land, the snow, the episodes of calm and natural beauty after scenes of great violence and misery, are part of the story, which is arranged with a musical sense of fitness in the changes of mood. The whole truth about the experience of these years is to be built up gradually, and, partly for this reason, the first fifty pages of the novel are confused by the lack of a firm narrative. The reader is required to accept a series of impressions, not yet intelligibly related to each other, and a set of unexplained characters who are not clearly identified in his mind until much later. Pasternak does not even attempt the well-known virtues of the storyteller's art. He is writing a philosophical novel, a testimony of thought and experience, and not any kind of novel of character or of the fate of individuals. The villain is an abstract sketch of bourgeois corruption, and the story of his relations with the heroine is mere melodrama.

For this and other reasons any comparison between Pasternak and Tolstoy, either in intention or in effect, appears absurd from the very first page. One thinks of the swift, decisive beginning of Anna Karenina, the wonderful clarity and depth of the characters, and the impression left of the whole span of their lives lived in their natural circumstances. Not one of the characters in Doctor Zhivago, not even Zhivago himself, is endowed with this rounded naturalness, nor are their lives steadily unfolded before the reader. The novel moves forward in short paragraphs and in short episodes, which are all related by strings of coincidence to the central figure; he and the heroine, Lara, together carry the whole weight of the story, as the picture is formed of the old society collapsing and of the new one forming in confusion and terror. If any single

literary influence is to be mentioned, it seems to me that
the most prominent is Shakespeare. The influence appears
in the use of the wild dialogue of the characters of the
under-plot, in the short scenes that somehow, as in *Antony
and Cleopatra*, suggest the great events across great distances, and, above all, in the suggestion of signs of the
supernatural in the natural order. Pasternak's Russia can
contain witches and metaphysical fools alongside images
of ideal love escaping from a corruption, in which the
personalities and idiosyncrasies of the lovers and of the
villain play no part. There is something of Shakespeare,
whom Pasternak translated, in the sudden blending of the
imagery and the philosophical reflection, in the affinities
found between abstract thought and natural appearances.

It would be very gross and very dishonest to interpret
this novel as primarily a condemnation of Soviet Communism. About the author's intentions no mistake is
possible, since, like Proust, he clearly explains his philosophy in all its divisions, of aesthetics, politics, and
personal morality, both directly and in words attributed
to his characters. The Soviet State is indeed condemned
as a degeneration from the revolution, which was the
moment of liberty and of the assertion of the forces of life.
The revolution itself is represented as one of the few great
events of human history, comparable with the overthrow
of Roman power as the ancient world ended. The old
régime is shown as currupting personal life as deeply, if
less violently, than the Soviet fanaticism that succeeds it.
But ultimately political action and organisation are incidental to the most serious interests of men and women,
which are to be found in the sources of art and of religion.
These sources of renewal have been discovered, whenever

a man achieves some heightened sense of his own part in
the processes of life that makes his own death seem not a
final waste. Men arrive at this deliverance and rest, when
they have succeeded in communicating perfectly with one
other person, giving the testimony of their own experience, either in love or in a work of art. The inconsolable
people–Doctor Zhivago's wife and Lara's husband–are
those who have never shared their isolation. This sense
of the overwhelming need to communicate one's own
individual experience, to add something distinctive to the
always growing sum of the evidences of life, is the most
moving theme of the book. The political cruelties, the
crimes and errors of the Soviet system, are not made into
grounds for final pessimism, and are certainly not the
grounds for hopes of counter-revolution or of salvation
from the West.

There are several long passages that read like a memory
of the early writings of Hegel, particularly two in which
Pasternak repeats Hegel's account of the historical rôle of
Christianity in creating the modern man, who need no
longer be either master or slave. For him Russia, the
country in which people 'talk as only Russians talk', is
plainly the leading nation of this century, and, staying at
home and somehow keeping alive the radical traditions
of the Russian intelligentsia, he has written a work of
universal significance, which offers hope and encouragement. The vindication of the freedom of art, and of private
life lived on the appropriate human scale, does not appear
in this novel as the conventional and now frigid liberalism
of the West. There is no suggestion of nervous fence-
building, of the shrill, defensive note of those who live
within a stockade, trying not to notice the movements

outside, by which they know that their fate is being decided.

Written in proud isolation, *Dr. Zhivago* will, I think, always be read as one of the most profound descriptions of love in the whole range of modern literature.

16

Proust – I

I T is impossible that there should be any simple relation
between *A la Recherche du Temps Perdu* and the story
of Proust's life. Proust's discovery, as he believed it to be,
of the true relation of art to life, was to him the most
important event of his own life, strictly analogous to a
religious conversion. It was the discovery of the meaning
of his existence, and his true destiny, after a long wandering in the desert. The desert was Society, in every possible
meaning of that term. The novel has the form of a testa-
ment, which tells the story of the narrator-pilgrim's
search for truth through the false hopes and diversions in
the desert up to the final revelation. From the beginning
it is consistently written in accordance with the philosophical principles, of which the discovery is to be the
climax of the book.

These principles require that only a 'creative autobiography' (Mr. Painter's phrase in *Marcel Proust: A
Biography*[1]), written in resolute solitude, can give the
essence of any man's life, which is to be found in his
unique mode of feeling and of perceiving. Behind the
straightforward narrative, the log-book of observable and
successive events and of conscious purposes, there lies a
significant design, to which we can have access only
through the constructive imagination fed by unconscious
memory. This buried music of recurring themes gives the

[1] Chatto & Windus, 1966 and 1967.

true laws of an individual's development, the essence of a particular personality. This is the reality of which the phenomena recorded in the definitive biography are only the blurred signs. The individual essence of Proust's mind and sensibility cannot be communicated by any biographer, and, according to Proust, a biographer would fall into the Sainte-Beuve fallacy if he tried to explain the character of the work by the story of Proust's life and of its historical circumstances. The story of his life is indeed part of the history of the times. History has its uses, and the greatest of them is to provide material for an individual's imagination to work on later. But *l'expérience vécue*, an individual's mode of consciousness, is not to be found in the history of his time. A literal summary of external events can never be a true account of that which any individual saw and felt; this truth can only be communicated in the metaphors and images and fictions that he himself will recognize with a shock of sudden pleasure as his own, and as answering to his own peculiar sensibility. The real life of a person can only be represented by imaginative parody of the subject's characteristic style of speech and writing and movement, if not by the subject's own shaping of his involuntary memories into the forms of art. Parody was the beginning of Proust's own gift as a writer; indeed he was a brilliant parodist and mimic when, before the philosophical discovery, he was still without any kind of formed style and method of construction of his own. After the discovery, he created the world of social comedy around the pilgrim, Marcel, by the exercise of the comedian's gift of absorbing alien personalities. Alone among his gifts as a writer, this came to him from nature, and not from the mature philosophy that his incredible will later translated into a new didactic form of fiction. Even for the exercise of this natural gift he found a philosophical justification. All art is parody, and the supreme art is self-parody, the concentration in some satisfying form of one's own hitherto unconscious, and apparently trivial, irrationalities of fantasy. The rational element in feeling and behaviour is always superficial and cannot be the material of art; for art is concerned only with that which is individual and which cannot be directly stated in general terms.

Proust's philosophy required *A la Recherche* to reproduce the essential 'laws' of the author's individual consciousness, the irrational themes and cross-references that from the beginning shaped his relationships in love, his friendships, his perceptions, and his style. If Proust can find the fitting form for the recurring themes of his own consciousness, the reader will both enter into Proust's world, which must be unlike any other, and he will at the same time be shown the only way into his own individual consciousness, past the barriers of habit and of stock response and of social convention. Art is the expression of these involuntarily recurring patterns within individual consciousness, and our response to art is a recognition of similarly discoverable, but characteristically different, submerged rhythms within ourselves. Proust despised aestheticism and formalist theories of art, doctrines that are comforting only to the idle and unproductive connoisseurs, to '*les célibataires de l'art*'. His philosophy makes art essentially cognitive, an uncovering of a kind of truth that cannot be discovered by any rational method. The essential virtue of a serious novelist, painter, or musician is a persevering truthfulness, a loyalty to the unexplained details of moving significance that he finds within his experience, when he disregards everything that is habitual, rational, and socially conditioned in his own perceptions. Like Schopenhauer, Proust uses the language of Platonic Ideas, which can be perceived by a child or an artist, peering with an exaggerated curiosity at the flux of his experience, when the will to act is morbidly relaxed. It follows that the biographer of an artist, and in particular of Proust, is committed to reversing this process of artistic creation, and to restoring all the accidental features of the subject's experience which he in his work had winnowed away.

Mr. Painter's first volume, and particularly its earlier chapters, are indeed a fascinating demonstration in reverse of the working of Proust's imagination, In the unobtrusively learned reconstruction of the scenes and names around Illiers, we are for the first time given the full prose sources of the philosophical poetry of Swann and of the Guermantes Way. Gradually, comparing the accidents of Proust's experience with the essence that he extracted from it, one begins to see exactly where the peculiar stresses and distortions of his imaginative reconstruction fall.

First, he always saw people and scenes, and his own moods and passions, with a microscopic intensity. The normal, middle-distance view of human comedy is altogether lacking in the novel, and is restored in the biography. The effect of this magnifying-glass intensity is that there can be no true picture in the novel of human beings purposefully doing things, engaged in the common business of their professions, or pursuing definite purposes. There is no account of sustained action, or of any planned achievement, anywhere in the novel. Secondly, the normal dimension of time has to be removed. Proust has therefore no use for a plot as an organizing principle; for a plot presents a personality through the history of its activities, and this is no less superficial than mere psychological analysis, which was the fashinable principle of fiction in his time. One can now see why it was a condition of the full development of Proust's sensibility that he should spend his life among the professionally idle and frivolous, in Society, and that he should at all costs escape from his father's active, and responsible, professional world. His characters must live and develop as a plant lives and develops, according to some secret law of growth, putting out new fronds of self-expression. They are caught under close observation at different times, but they can never be seen from a distance in the steady trajectory of their continuous activities and reasonable aims. Proust's own favourite and marvellous metaphors in describing personal, and particularly sexual, life are botanical metaphors. His characters are attracted to each other, interwine and destroy each other, with the monstrous and irresistible luxuriance of tropical plants. We never see them moving, but we find them in new postures as we walk up and down the great conservatory.

Mr. Painter restores in his biography the personalities of Parisian society whom Proust transfigured, by making from his memories and mimicry of them that strange jungle world of bizarre attraction and interleavings that is at once comical and repellent. There can be no doubt that Proust's art passes the test that he imposed upon all art: we have a far more vivid sense of the permanent and inescapable reality of the fictional characters–particularly of Charlus, Bloch, and Saint-Loup–than of any single one of Mr. Painter's shadowy figures of lighter social comedy.

Perhaps the competition between art and history is not being quite fairly tested, since a Frenchman could probably do more to make such people as Lucien and Léon Daudet, Barrès, Montesquiou, Reynaldo Hahn, Anna de Noailles, Jacques-Émile Blanche, Madame Straus, seem real and interesting. But even when every allowance is made for an English biographer's willed, and also his involuntary, remoteness from the social scene that he describes, the density and permanence of the social milieu created by Proust from these scattered materials is astonishing. The great gap between *Jean Santeuil*, which is largely incompetent, uncertain, and formless as a work of art, and *A la Recherche*, is explained by Proust himself in *Le Temps Retrouvé*. Before his philosophical discovery, he had no means of fusing the particular and the general in a single design. The imaginative memories and the general reflections lie side by side, 'like an object with a price-label attached to it'.

There is no comparable instance in modern literature of a writer discovering his own genius, late in life, through the discovery of a theory of the mind and of personality, and then exercising this genius, and illustrating the theory, by representing his earlier, uncreative life as a progress under destiny towards this discovery. It is as if the insights and the intellectual excitement to be found in Flaubert's letters had been woven into the texture of *Madame Bovary*, or of *L'Éducation Sentimentale*, instead of their being merely applied in these works. We cannot find the minds of Flaubert and of Stendhal, in their full range, completely expressed in their fiction; we have also to read Flaubert's letters and *La Vie de Henri Brulard*. Their own understanding of the sources and significance of their own fiction is to be found outside it, and is not absorbed within the work itself as a necessary part of its picture of experience. That Proust's letters should be found for the most part trivial and disappointing is one more evidence of the supreme strategy of his life, of his patience and cunning as an artist.

In general the more theory-laden fiction of the last century, and particularly Tolstoy's, gives an inadequate, and even falsified, picture of human existence because it omits both the sources and the value of its own creation. The moral values conveyed are thereby made more simple and unambiguous than they were in Tolstoy's own experience. This is the dishonesty of fiction. We cannot really be decived by the rhetoric of 'Madame Bovary, c'est moi', or be persuaded to identify spoiled romanticism with the labouring self-consciousness, and with the passion for style and form, which so painfully put together the essential image of it. The work that made the picture cannot be allowed to have no place in the picture itself. Proust himself expressly noticed the added depths of works of art that represent also the conditions of their own creation. He felt a particular affinity with Vermeer, who painted the artist seated at his easel, bathed in the light that he must represent, with a mirror beyond him, reflecting the scene. This poetry of inner and answering reflections, and of self-commentary, gives his novel its strength and density, its life-like completeness and two-facedness. The gap between the work of reconstructing experience and experience itself has been closed by showing their common source in the hidden depths of the narrator's fantasies and involuntary memories, and by showing his progress, step by step, towards realizing in a transparent form the submerged patterns in his consciousness, which alone have given some unity to his otherwise dissipated life.

The validity of this aesthetic philosophy, and its success in application, have become easier to appreciate after reading the first volume of this biography. We can at last try to separate that which is due to aesthetic principle and that which is due to accidents of temperament and circumstance. We may for the first time judge why Proust fell short (if it is to be admitted that he did) of the full universality at which he aimed through the disengagement of the essential themes in his own life.

The limiting weakness seems to me his inability to represent the enjoyment of action and the normal rhythms of experience with its natural human continuity. In *Le Temps Retrouvé*, rationalising the peculiarity of his own passive temperament, he suggests that action, and the need for action, are marks of mediocrity of mind. At this point he is gratefully accepting the philosophies of Schopenhauer and Bergson, against Taine and Zola, and against naturalists and positivists of all kinds, who were no less his enemies than the contemporary aesthetes and formalists. But are the sensuous passivity of the narrator in love and jealousy, his intent listening to the slight movements of ebb and flow in his own consciousness, really the idiosyncrasies only of a man who is always lying in a bed of sickness, either in fact or in his own imagination? The narrator is from the beginning a sleepless observer, peering at the spectacle before him, enclosed within a vegetable, trance-like world of dreams and drugs, in which the crisis is always a moment of hyperaesthesia, a lapse into some special lucidity, and is never an escape from solipsism, except finally in his work. Apart from declaring himself a Dreyfusard, the narrator has only one adult decision to make, as a free agent, and that is the decision finally to write. This is atonement for his fateful decision as a child to call and keep his mother in his room at night, when the guests came, and so to yield to the anxiety that would prevent him from being active and that would prepare him for his vocation. Mr. Painter in his second volume reviews the evidence about the nature and effects of Proust's illness, on which some work has been done in France. *'Les malades se sentent plus près de leur âme'* were Proust's own words. But there is a certain degree of presence of soul, and absence of the sense of physical circumstance, which makes some pages of *A la Recherche* seem more like a casebook study than a general truth about experience presented in a poetical and concrete image. The animal soul, man as a coarse sanguine physical agency, so real in Tolstoy, does not appear at all alongside the vegetative and intellectual parts of the soul. Therefore the whole of Nature becomes insubstantial and emblematic, a diaphanous veil through which spiritual truths can be discerned. There is nothing real outside the single room, except the view from the window, perhaps of Gilberte's snow in the Champs-Élysées, or the noises that come through the walls in the early morning with their message of the unattainable sunlight outside.

Proust's society surrounded an efflorescence of varied genius in the arts, perhaps the greatest efflorescence that Europe has seen since the Renaissance. Like Henry James in England, Proust saw both its corruption and its vindication, as he thought, in the stupid waste and in the heroism of the Great War, and, towards the end of *A la Recherche*, he began consciously to write its epitaph, in the form of a

Comédie Humaine. Reading his life, and then restudying the novel, one is at many points forced to acknowledge elements that are untranslatably French, and not relevant to England, in Proust's judgment on society and on the place of art and of the artist in society. The general truth in its concrete image is sometimes very particularly French. Class divisions had different origins in the two countries, and the role of the aristocracy, and therefore the varieties of snobbery, were correspondingly different; and a purely French literary heritage had formed Proust's style and vision. When he was moved to tears by George Eliot and Thomas Hardy, he may have found the picture of society in their novels almost as poetically strange as in the *Arabian Nights*.

That which is untranslatably French in Proust's own vision comes from the tradition of the French moralists, which formed the main line of French fiction, as the example of Shakespeare formed the main line of English fiction. It is essential to this moralists' tradition that it takes, first, the Court, and then its bourgeois successor, the drawing-room, as the contexts in which the essence of human nature is displayed: and, connectedly, the problem of human nature, and therefore the proper subject of fiction, is human vanity, that despairing word which echoes through French prose from Pascal to Proust. For two centuries the standard subject of French fiction had been the essence and metamorphoses of human vanity in love and in politics. The essential action takes place within four walls, with the hero either arriving painfully at true self-knowledge, or, as engineer of his fate, playing upon that intricate mechanism of vanity which is the universal principle of motion in society, as gravitation is in the material world. Although he extends its range and adds depth to its conclusions, Proust remains unalterably part of this moralists' tradition, the Saint-Simon of bourgeois society, as he recognized, who had to find the extravagant vanities, and the casual cruelties, of the Court in the drawing-rooms of Paris. The famous, sometimes tedious, phenomenon of snobbism, as it appears in Proust, is the descendant of contested Court precedence surviving in a capitalist and mobile society, and the reversal of social values at the end of the novel follows closely the rise of the bastards in Saint-Simon. The narrator's own deliverance from love and from social ambition, and his redemption through art, is one more version, and a deeper one, of the classical hero's escape from vanity into self-knowledge, the theme that is endlessly repeated in French literature from the seventeenth century onwards.

It is possible in some moods to feel stifled within the four walls of self-examination, and to be unconvinced by these always gleeful probings of the varieties of human vanity. It is possible to regard Courts, and born courtiers like Proust, as brilliant aberrations, and to look for more various scenes for full self-expression elsewhere and not in the metamorphoses of high society at all. Much of English fiction has taken the Puritan and Protestant family, away from Court and courtiers, attached to its locality and possessions, as a natural scene of human self-expression, and the act of marriage, the foundation of a family, as one illustrative centre of any human story. It is possible also to demand that fiction, when it is most ambitious, should never be too concentrated upon a single theme or situation, but should rather be dissipated by incidents and allusions that will show something of an uncontrolled natural and social order outside the window, away from the individual consciousness, in an open country. These are reservations that arise immediately from any Englishman's experience of literature, whether he chooses to suppress them or not. He may also find Proustian snobbism, descended from the snobbism of courtly precedence and protocol, remote from the familiar English snobbery, in which the successive layers of aristocracy have been generally less significant than the many degrees of distinction, obscurely and locally recognized along many different scales. He may therefore finally turn from Proust to Turgenev, Chekhov, and Tolstoy, to pictures of a society that was in reality even more unlike his own, and yet find their representation of men's natural conditions and purposes, their moral anxieties, their distrust of intellect and formality, their seeming untidiness and indefiniteness of mood and feeling, their religious sense of Nature, nearer to his experience and education in many respects than anything in Proust, except the scenes of childhood. The difference between the two national traditions in fiction is partly a difference between forms of social life, and of religion, in the two countries, even if it is also a difference of aesthetic principles. But neither of these factors is independent of the other, and biography can show the relations between them.

17

⋘ ⋙

Proust — II

IN the second volume of his biography Mr. George
Painter subordinates the story of Proust's life to the
story of the composition of the novel, as Proust increasingly subordinated his living to his writing, until he was
scarcely alive at all, except in the re-creation of his own
past. Mr. Painter dwells upon the most trivial recorded
fact, if it will throw light on the text of the novel. He
otherwise abbreviates the story of friendships and of
society, which he had set himself to recount in the first
volume.

He shows the importance of the various versions of
Contre Sainte-Beuve as dividing stages in Proust's thought,
and as clearing the ground for *Le Temps Retrouvé*. One
can follow, in convincing detail, the building, layer upon
layer of extravagance in digression, of the final style and
vision. The problem had been to see exactly how the
immense gap between *Jean Santeuil*, a formless and insipid
work of pathos, and *Swann* was filled in; Mr. Painter
shows exactly how, and by what false starts and discarded
fragments the first structure of the novel was built. It was
a dramatic necessity for Proust to represent his conversion
to his mature philosophy as a Cartesian revelation. But
the revelation extended over years of stylistic experiment.

During the years of revision and amplification of *A La
Recherche*, from 1913 to 1922, Proust was living within
his novel, converting his own experience, as it unrolled,

into fiction which had less and less the appearance of fiction. The evocations of the beauty of wartime Paris during air-raids, the description of the narrator's visits to the brothel, of the Dreyfusards becoming patriots and the anti-Dreyfusards becoming defeatists, the praise of the greatness of France, the condemnation of aesthetes who wanted to risk soldiers' lives to preserve churches–these are among the passages that gave the novel a new depth. It becomes Balzacian in range, a review of a passing social order and of a civilization faltering. He was commemorating the last phase, as it seemed, of the most glorious period in the history of civilization since the Renaissance. The darkness of wartime Paris in the novel has its equivalent in the darkness of Proust's wartime life, and of his night-town visitations. He becomes in these years a figure from the *Arabian Nights*; sick and muffled, he moves from palace to hovel, prying and searching for extremes of curious pleasure, cruelty, and suffering. He had an increasing sense of social life as a phantasmagoria of disguises, in which every sexual and social combination is somewhere realised.

It is difficult, perhaps impossible, to know whether Mr. Painter has penetrated Proust's own sexual disguises. He does deny that Albertine was simply a transposition of a man into a woman, but he gives biographical grounds for this denial which seem still to leave the issue in some doubt. Like Maurois before him, he has shown that experimental cruelty, and delight in at least the idea of a descent into the nethermost underworld, was a fact in Proust's life as in his imagination. 'We must never be afraid to go too far, because truth lies beyond' was a saying of Proust's. Only in extremes of degradation and of goodness can the truth about the ambivalences of passion be found. The advance that he hoped to make beyond his master, Balzac, was to show these extremes united in a single experience, not divided among opposing characters. He made the demonstration, not only in the invention of Charlus and Françoise, but in his own life. As in Proust's correspondence, so also in Mr. Painter's story, the sweetness and the cruelty are coiled around each other; Proust watches, traps, helps, beseeches, and eludes his friends and his servants. The war years seemed even darker and more sinister in Maurois' version of them.

Proust's theory of art in general, and of his own art, is finally in full view. Is the theory tenable? Is it vindicated by the novel itself, a work of 'moral poetry', as Proust himself described it? One has to start from the fact that his philosophy of art was rooted in his own pathological condition, and that he knew this, and made a virtue of this knowledge, with the claim that all original philosophies are the elaboration of pathological needs which determine an individual mode of vision. Proust suffered from hyperaesthesia, an illness, or abnormality, of mind and body, which he had to make into an instrument for ordering and mastering experience, rather than an excuse for succumbing under its weight. He had taken Ruskin as his master, because Ruskin had lent a moral significance to aesthetic attitudes which would otherwise be detached, heartless and trivial, without their power to redeem, and to give dignity to, ordinary existence. On the basis of a not dissimilar displacement of feeling from persons to perceptions, Ruskin had constructed an 'idolatry' (Proust's word for it) of works of art and of natural forms, and had made of the perception of physical detail a kind of worship.

Proust left Ruskin behind when he saw that the special object, the work of art, provides the occasion on which a man may revive authentic experience, a private real world, which is concealed by habit but which is always in principle recoverable. As an amateur he had used works of art as sounding devices, which echoed his own unconscious memories and returned them to him. In his conscious mind he could hear the echo, but not the original, which is normally lost to a man at the moment of his expulsion from childhood. An aesthetic experience is authentic in so far as it is a discovery of the recurring themes which distinguish one man's perceptions from everyone else's, and which hold together his private world, and form his style of expression. Aesthetic experience is therefore always self-discovery, and the gradual invention of a fitting style is the most complete and clear form of self-discovery.

When he had arrived at this theory of art, at the conclusion of *Contre Sainte-Beuve*, Proust had accepted the corollary that any formal criticism of literature, and any accepted canons of style and structure for the novel, are delusive; originality is the only value in literature, and parody is the only valid criticism. 'We must make an intentional pastiche in order not to spend the rest of our lives in writing involuntary pastiche,' he concluded. Most art at any time is involuntary pastiche, and more fundamentally, most men's lives and speech are a pastiche of the dominating models of the time. The solitary, unhistorical self is released only by some extravagance of self-will and by withdrawal, and sometimes also by the accident of perversion; so Charlus gradually becomes an appropriate hero of Proust's novel. Proust cunningly divided his own attributes between the narrator and Charlus, relieving his work of the burden of being a direct confession of the author's guilt and of his destructive rages. The narrator is represented as having redeemed the egoism and cruelty of his life by a work which shows the necessity of his sufferings as a way to enlightenment. But this is not the whole story, and it would be too complacent and consoling if it were. Charlus declines and dies, vicious and unconsoled, in spite of his goodness, while mediocrity flourishes around him.

The doctrine that literature returns us to the themes of an inner world, which is the only reality that we can fully explore, entails that the objects referred to in society and in the naturalistic novel are an unstable compromise; they are not in themselves worth re-creating directly. Suppose this is conceded: a difficulty still remains, which leads to a familiar criticism of the later parts of the novel, at least from *La Prisonnière* onwards. The dissolution of the common world of shared experiences, and the picturing of love and friendship as illusions, make it difficult for a writer to show in relief those themes that constitute his individual sense of reality. He will seem to force the reader to see things as he does, and will leave him too little to do for himself, in finding the connections and implications that are particularly significant to him. In the last four volumes one may feel imprisoned, like Albertine with the narrator, within the enveloping, annihilating consciousness of Proust, always sleepless and active in making his points, a writer who does not relent and let go. He comes near to smothering all differences in the external world beneath the uniform texture and rhythm of his style, the rhythms of his coiling, spiralling mind. The sounds from the street outside come faintly into the room in which not only he, but the enthralled reader also, sometimes suffocates. One sometimes wants to escape from the immobilities of the style and to see independent objects again, as in *Swann* and in the earlier social comedy. In the terrible last years, Proust could no longer, in his despairing hurry, allow his themes to emerge indirectly, and by implication, for fear that the structure of the whole work would not be seen, and that the complex message would vanish. He still thought that he might possibly lose his long race against Time.

18

◄◄ ►►

Edmund Burke

Iᴛ is difficult to be fair to Burke, and to distinguish
rhetoric from thought in his speeches and writing, if
he is made a mere weapon in contemporary politics. He
has first to be returned to his proper setting, alongside
Hume, Johnson and Sir Joshua Reynolds, if his intentions
and his limits are to be truthfully recognised. He was not
a systematic thinker with an original philosophy of
politics, comparable with Rousseau and Bentham and
J. S. Mill. But he did confront the facts of revolution, and
the necessity of reform, with a set of unanalysed ideas,
ideas that have been echoed in English oratory ever since
and that still retain an uncertain power. The selection
from Burke under review[1] has an introduction which
confidently enlists him in the Cold War. The confidence,
though irritating, is not misplaced; he will indeed serve.
But the advantage of reading him is thereby missed. He
has more to say about present issues less crudely defined;
and the selection itself is fair enough to show this.

In almost every year since the last war ended, there has
been argument about the legitimate scope of political
action: about means and ends. How many eggs can
justifiably be broken, and under what conditions, with a
view to making an omelette of some approved social
consistency? The Jacobins introduced this now familiar

[1] *The Philosophy of Edmund Burke.* Edited by Louis Bredvold and
Ralph Ross. Cresset Press, 1961.

idea (but not the ugly metaphor) of politics as essentially omelette-making, and therefore as necessarily egg-breaking. The Cuban revolution, and contrary attitudes towards it, started the argument again, as has every recent movement of revolutionary nationalism. 'Of course there is great injustice, tyranny and persecution: but so there was before, and in the long run . . .' Burke knew and hated this now familiar Jacobin form of apology: the argument from the long run. He also knew that, once admitted, it would be horribly persuasive. It is worth examining his reasons.

'Art is man's nature.' This is the centre of his thought. He had to start from the idea of Nature, because every thinker of his century, and particularly his enemies, had started there. The idea of the stripped, natural man, liberated from the draperies of convention and of obedience, had guided the Jacobins and the philosophical radicals. In this ancient and simple picture Nature and Convention, or Manners, are true opposites, contrasted as innocence and corruption, and as equality and difference. Nature is something to which you can return for renewal, in the way that in *As You Like It* the court is refreshed in the forest.

Consistently and throughout his life, Burke strove to reverse this picture. That which is distinctively human in men, and therefore their nature, flows from the conventions and manners, from the imposed style of life, which over the years have formed their moral sentiments and manners. The 'natural affections' are inseparable from urbanity, from the softened manners only learnt in a social order. As Hume had suggested without further elaboration, nature operates upon man through a second nature, custom, as it operates upon the brutes through instinct. Men can never return to instinctual freedom and to primal innocence, and discover rights that are founded in some original and universal endowment. Every right that they sincerely feel to be theirs, whether in India, France, or the American Colonies, has its intimate setting in the time-honoured culture that formed them.

Whenever they are goaded, either by false philosophy or by oppression, to tear down the civil order and to look for a natural order beneath it, they will finally return to the harsher customs of their primitive past, and not to an original innocence. Under intolerable strain they may regress from adult habits to the childhood of their history. But they cannot escape into a pre-social world, into an Eden of instinct, which is altogether outside history. The natural affections of men are never the biological attractions and repugnances of a naked creature in a forest. They have been formed at every stage by the successive institutions which clothed men with moral ideas.

In Europe, but not in India, these institutions descend from Christianity, and from the orators, moralists and lawyers of the ancient world. If at any time Europeans are oppressed by the civil order, and want to be stripped of their corruptions, they will naturally return to their formative past, and particularly to the ancient world, to the classical origins of their institutions. In the aesthetics of the eighteenth century, it is familiar that the return to the classical past was often taken as the equivalent of a return to Nature. Posed in classical drapery by a tree in a great park, with a Palladian house in the distance, the family group is a true picture of humanity in its natural and permanent condition, Such a picture, painted by Reynolds or by Gainsborough, was the equivalent of Burke's vision of politics. The naturalness and the artificiality are two sides of the same coin.

Outside civil society human nature knows nothing that makes it human. The state of civil society, which generates an aristocracy of one kind or another, is the true State of Nature. The great estates, and the civil order itself, were originally obtained by violence. But it is old violence, and their long establishment has improved the original instincts into moral habits and into respect for positive law. To quote the first and distant usurpation as a justification of present violence is always a political fallacy, a misconception of law and therefore of justice, with frightening echoes of the Civil War.

The only touchstone for reform in politics is–does this measure on the whole accord with the natural affections of men, as reflected in their present moral sentiments and their manner of living at this time? If, concerned with freedom in colonial territories, we ask what a free government is, the only answer is–it is what the people concerned think is free: they are the only proper and competent judges in this matter. Any abstract dissection of freedom, or of some allegedly original and common needs of men, is irrelevant. Political wisdom, which Burke, after Aristotle, called prudence, is the quick recognition of formed, and in this sense, artificial, expectations of freedom and of justice, as they exist at any particular place at any particular time. These expectations are historical facts, not metaphysical ideals, and they are to be understood only through their historical causes.

It follows that we must always do wrong if, as radicals, we engage in political arithmetic, and plan the general improvement of mankind over hundreds and thousands of years, overriding all local differences. Such a plan must presuppose an impossible science of original and stripped human nature, a science that is independent of historical understanding. It presupposes also a morality that is independent of 'utility', as interpreted by particular men at particular times. The true utility of any social change must depend on the artificially formed tastes and prejudices of those immediately affected by it. Statesmen who disregard prejudices, and existing standards of justice, in the interests of an abstract ideal, succeed only in undermining morality and law by destroying their customary associations. By exposing the artificiality of social conventions, they turn every conflict of interest into a conflict of wills, unmediated by commonly respected restraints. Once this has happened, we shall try continuously to re-make society, as we go along, counting each man only as an ally or an enemy to our own conceptions. This is the effect of the Jacobin arithmetic of perpetual revolution: continuously count eggs and break just as many as are required for the imagined omelette.

Burke's rhetoric was mere assertion. It was not proof or even argument. He was not clear and he was not consistent. He saw less far into the future than the philosophical radicals and the men of the Enlightenment, less far certainly than Condorcet. He had a confused and superstitious idea of providence within history. He was often merely reactionary and frightened. But some part of his conclusions, freely interpreted, may still be relevant and true.

The principle of political arithmetic can be tested by an example: it might be said (and sometimes is) that the abolition of capital punishment is a comparatively trivial issue, since the happiness of comparatively few individuals and families is at stake. This is arithmetic: why is it a gross mistake in this application? The deliberate taking of a man's life is an enormous act, which reminds us of the most primitive prohibition of a primitive impulse. It is part of the foundation of morality itself, and of any form of civil existence, that this enormity should be directly felt as such. In most societies there will be some prescribed conditions in which the original horror is by convention mitigated; in ours, conspicuously, in war, and in capital punishment for murder. One kind of progress consists in challenging these conventional mitigations one by one, as we travel further from the original necessities, and from the helplessness, out of which the prescribed exceptions arose. An argument about capital punishment is therefore recognized on both sides to be an argument that touches the first foundations of morality.

There seems to be a strange inconsistency between feeling intensely the evil of capital punishment and feeling weakly the evil of freely taking lives, as a matter of policy, for the sake of economic and social improvements. Yet it is not unusual to find these apparently inconsistent attitudes combined in the same radical minds. Why? Perhaps because killing, and unlawful imprisonment, as an incident in social revolution, have in many places been institutionalised, alongside war and capital punishment. Perpetual revolution, therefore, is accepted as 'natural', in the only effective and Burkean sense of this word.

Political arithmetic, now a habit, has served to loosen the established ideas of common morality in order to establish a new Jacobin sense of justice, which is akin to the ancient morality of war. Perpetual revolutionaries, and their apologists, see their acts as forming the future through some direct consequences which justify them. They will not see them as also forming the future as precedents. Yet, inconsistently, they will generally quote the violence of the past as justification for their violence in the present. They are then, in fact, arguing from precedent to precedent, and are appealing in part to custom and prescriptive rights, even though they have repudiated these Burkean notions.

To judge policies solely by their direct effects is the false notion of utility. If, as Burke believed, men derive their natural affections, and their sense of justice and of freedom, from a long chain of respected customs, and always within an institutional frame, it must be wrong not to judge policies by the precedents that are established in their execution. An act of injustice, or an unusual outrage (like the use of atomic weapons), may sometimes seem justified by its consequences as evidently a lesser evil. But the mere fact that the act has been officially performed will need also to be counted among the consequences, through its operation on the future as a precedent, and therefore ultimately as a permission.

This is Burke's case against Jacobinism, and against the ideal of perpetual revolution. This eighteenth-century picture of the urbane, institutional man has its relevance, no less than the opposing and contemporary picture of rustic innocents, unspoiled by kings and priests. Perhaps they both need to be kept on permanent exhibition together.

19

◄◄ ►►

George Eliot's Essays

W RITING for the *Westminster* or for the *Leader*, a radical weekly that George Henry Lewes had helped to found, George Eliot was under no pressure to be amusing, or to catch the attention of distracted readers. In the 1850s a literary essay or book review was addressed to a public accustomed from childhood to listen to sermons. The essay, as a kind of lay sermon, had a very different form and purpose from the modern review, which must compete for time and attention with the news. The difference is partly one of pace, but, more subtly, one of confidence. George Eliot could assume that men and women, often separated by quiet, uncrossed distances in the country, and yet conscious of themselves as forming the thinking public, would attend gratefully to her slow argument and to its evidences. They would not need to be entertained, sentence by sentence and paragraph by paragraph, by an anxious author who, like a cabaret performer, has his bright eye always fixed upon his audience to detect the first sign of restlessness. Her readers would stay with her until the end, waiting for the sober truth and for her summing-up. One can measure in her Essays[1] the progress we have made towards a widely diffused brightness and vulgarity in literary journalism, with its compensating gains and losses.

The most evident of our losses is in clarity and definite-

[1] Edited by Thomas Pinney. Routledge, 1963.

ness of statement. Whether Heine or Tennyson, Carlyle
or a famous popular preacher, Goethe or German Philosophy, are under review, George Eliot tries in each essay
to arrive at a just evaluation by reasoning which the
reader cannot fail to follow. There is no allusiveness or
decorative diversion. She has a doctrine to establish and
is at pains not to be misunderstood. Her principles of
criticism were simple in themselves, but immensely
difficult to apply to particular cases. I will try to state her
principles.

The value of literature, whether poetry or fiction, consists in the truthful representation, first, of human feeling,
and, secondly, of the underlying moral order. Under the
first heading the office of any considerable writer is to
extend human sympathy; under the second, to suggest, or
to convey in some manner appropriate to the medium, a
just proportion between the proper objects of human
feeling. Falseness, coldness, artificiality, abstractness—these
are the corrupting vices of pseudo-literature, and he who
exhibits tnem, like Young of *Night Thoughts*, fails by this
first test. The editor, quoting Humphry House, finds a
Wordsworthian standard implied in this, and also in the
second test—that of truthfulness in presenting the natural
objects of feeling in due proportion.

Behind this resemblance there is a complicating difference. George Eliot believed that there must be a natural
history of human manners, a kind of moral biology.
The evolution of morals, no less than the origin of species,
follows discernible laws. There are necessary phases, and
necessary subordinations also, in the natural progress of
society; and rational inquiry, a responsible social science,
will be a guide to the true morality. Into the connotation

of 'natural', therefore, there enters another, unWords-worthian significance: for naturalness and truth of feeling are contrasted not only with the artificiality and conventions of urbane public manners, but also with distortions of the true moral development of society. There is a natural justice, a permanent order, to be discerned beneath changing social arrangements; imagination in fiction and poetry may reveal this order. Certainly poetry, and fiction, are false, and flawed as literature, if they misrepresent the due relation between the permanent moral order and the passing forms of contemporary society. Tennyson's 'Maud' was harshly derided in an anonymous review in the *Westminster* for its morbid misrepresentation of social fact, and of true social values. The weight of the charge was not that the poem was inexpressive, and that no genuine feeling was conveyed, but rather that the feeling conveyed was in conflict with the developing moral order, was reactionary, and depended upon false beliefs: peaceful, engrossing merchants are not to be vilified in comparison with a supposed chivalrous and warlike past. There could be no memorable justice in poetic language and in expression where they are associated with such false, tinsel thinking, which is at best only the pretty rhetoric of the emotions.

This aesthetic of truthfulness, and the pride in intelligence that goes with it, are very impressive: also the unity of tone, the confidence, the conscientious clarity, the fact that the critic so evidently knows where she stands and will not shuffle, or try to please, or unwittingly make an exception and thereby fall into inconsistency. The trouble (as it seems now) is: how are the truths of the moral order discerned? How are the natural objects of human feeling discriminated, if not in aesthetic experience itself? What is moral biology?

George Eliot was of course not a cold, Comtean positivist, but rather was strongly moved by a natural piety towards social fact. She believed that the great central movement of history, the march of mind, in her century, and particularly in Germany, would surely carry us into the upper air of more refined sympathies. As an amateur sociologist, she looked at social relations as a Victorian naturalist would look at a seashell, or at a flower in a cranny, as minute evidence, and as a subtle deposit, of the grand process of nature at work.

The beauty of the concrete particular thing–or of a given institution or custom–and the beauty of any careful representation of it, lie in its suggestion of the wider whole of which it is part, as being a footstep left behind by nature on its way toward the higher forms, the forms of civilized human life. George Eliot's naturalism, her warmth and (often) delicacy in rendering details of custom and manners, was inspired by a Victorian variant of Spinozism, a piety towards the microcosm in which Natura Naturans can be understood. A whole social landscape can be imagined around her details. She more than once rejects with special disdain the old untruth that moral principle is, either logically or psychologically, dependent on one or other Christian theology. The essays convey a metaphysical faith, or at least a metaphysical emotion, fused with her moral and social philosophy. The sympathy that literature may engender is a sense of oneness with the order of created things, and has its ancestry in German metaphysics. Her belief in the poetry of literalness, of the prosaic representation of the ordinary conditions of existence, of the People, concretely imagined, was a philosophical belief.

Her sentiment of nature is revealed in the typical Victorian image of it. Of the shallow contrived poet whom she is belabouring, she writes:

> Place him on a breezy common, where the furze is in its golden bloom, where children are playing, and the horses are standing in the sunshine with fondling necks, and he would have nothing to say.

The common, the furze, the children, the horses, compose a Victorian engraving of a moralized, no longer wild naturalness, which places the natural and the human together, as it might be in the Home Counties, at Hampstead or Putney or Box Hill, near the homes of the London poets. How surprising it would be to find George Eliot writing: 'Place him in the Abyssinian desert, or in sight of the beasts of the jungle, and he would have nothing to say.' The scene before which the poet ought to have something to say is nearer home; the aesthetic and the domestic virtues are not very far apart. Nature herself is domesticated and ethically subdued, as in a Morland, and teaches a lesson.

George Eliot's commanding intelligence as a critic may not carry final conviction, it seems to me, because it works within these narrow and comfortable assumptions about the relations of art to morality, and of poetic to social values. Certain doubts would never suggest themselves to her. That human beings are unhappy animals, who deface their environment and spread ugliness and destruction around them, that they are an unstable accident of evolution, and that their transient and self-centred claim to a superior existence urgently requires justification – this is a possibility, a doubt, which her moral confidence provokes.

Humanism is an altogether unconvincing doctrine if it is so interpreted as to exclude this doubt. If Christian reassurances are really, and not in name only, discarded, the poetic values of the furze and the horses on the common – of an innocence at once cultivated and natural – may not be so easily linked with the literary values of the children inserted in this sentimentalised scene. Can we now, as good psychologists and moral biologists, have any reason to believe that the children and their play are appropriately innocent, and that they compose a harmonious and truthful picture with the other elements? One may still think that a poet ought to have something to say about the children and their play; but what he truthfully says may be far from the too soothing, too soft and peaceful, context of sunshine, furze and fondling horses.

20

A Composer's World

THE first four chapters of Hindemith's book, *A Composer's World*,[1] together with chapter 6 on 'Technique and Style', constitute a sustained and serious argument in aesthetics. Hindemith carefully (and often contemptuously) avoids many of the ordinary confusions of aesthetic theory; he distinguishes the situation of the audience from the situation of the composer and then considers the relation between them. He writes only of music; but much of his argument in these chapters is general and philosophical, and, if it is valid at all, will apply also to the arts other than music.

His starting-point seems to me indisputable; it is that music is to be taken seriously, as 'more than a pleasant play of sounds'. There is a recognized distinction between art and mere entertainment; and the principle of distinction is to be found in the situation of the audience, not in the intentions of the artist. Music is understood as art if, and only if, the listener is intellectually active in listening to it. If he remains intellectually passive and attends only to the surface play of sound, he is treating the music only as entertainment. The mental activity required of the listener is of a peculiar kind; his intellect and his imagery must to some extent work in parallel with the composer's; by a process of 'co-construction' he must find the structure of the work for himself. A musical impression is not an

[1] Harvard University Press, 1952.

impression passively received through the senses. The listener creates the impression in his own mind by tracing the structure of the work for himself, using his own natural imagery and his musical memory. If no such parallel working of the listener's mind is interesting, the work has failed as a work of art.

I think that the domain of art and of aesthetic enjoyment can be generally distinguished by this reference to the activity required of spectator or audience. 'Constructing in parallel' with painter or sculptor, the spectator must find for himself the various relations of forms involved, and without this activity one could not speak of his enjoyment as aesthetic enjoyment. It is for this reason that concepts such as 'structure' and 'rhythm' are naturally applied across all the arts; they have a direct meaning for us, because they refer to our own activity of following and anticipating the structure of a work while we look or listen. Aesthetic perception is active perception, in the sense that it involves reconstructing the elements of a design. It is a fact of experience that people derive intense satisfaction from this parallel tracing of a structure in the mind while looking and listening; particularly they derive satisfaction when the structure was in part anticipated, in part new.

It is natural, but also dangerous, to look for some explanation of this aspect of aesthetic enjoyment. It is dangerous because, where there is no experimental evidence, causal explanations are valueless; so much aesthetic theory has been vague psychology without evidence. It seems better to accept the fact and to leave the future scientist to explain. Hindemith, like Berenson and I. A. Richards before him, ignores the dangers of *a priori* psychology, and offers a theory which is vaguely suggestive in itself, and which interestingly reveals his own conservative attitude to his art. Our innate capacity for tracing musical structures must (he thinks) be derived from some common experiences. He looks therefore for the physiological basis of our understanding of musical structures, as Berenson looked for the physiological basis of our appreciation of pictorial forms. He finds the basis in common experiences of motion. He infers that there must be 'a primordial musical experience of a very primitive nature', upon which later musical experience is built; there must be 'structural prototypes', built in to our musical experience, and these structures persist in the memory, however sophisticated we become. These assumptions are unsupported by detailed evidence, but they are interesting because of the deductions that can be made from them. Hindemith concludes that structural experiments must always be confined within narrow bounds, if music is to be intelligible to the listener: 'We may conclude that there is . . . in principle never anything new in the general order, shape, and mutual relationship of musical successions. We may even go so far as to say that basically nothing new can ever be introduced into such successions, if we do not want to see the participant in music degraded to a dull, apathetic receptacle, an absorbent sponge reaching the point of saturation without showing any sign of reaction' (p. 20). Active listening must become impossible if wholly new structures are introduced. Unless the listener can follow, and to some extent anticipate, structure while he listens, the sounds are musically meaningless to him; and his ability to participate in this way depends on a common stock of natural musical imagery. Here again the argument seems to have a wider application; the intelligent perception of painting or sculpture depends upon there being stable units in the design, which can be matched in the spectator's own visual memory and in his own natural imagery; and the understanding of poetry depends upon the natural and acquired associations and ambiguities of words and of word rhythms. So much may be admitted, but still Hindemith's conservative conclusions do not follow; for the conclusions depend on his assumption that there are, in fact, 'structural prototypes' and 'primordial musical experiences', which set a final limit to the possible range of musical invention. His argument is not simply that new musical structures, if they are to be intelligible, must be evolved continuously from already familiar structures; he is not only defending tradition as the condition of experiment. He has a theory of innate and natural limits to invention, a theory based on the supposed psychology of listening.

Like most *a priori* psychologists, he assumes without evidence that understanding must involve having images. To understand or recognize a musical structure necessarily involves having a parallel structure of musical imagery in the mind. The composer must know that any listener's resources of musical imagery are limited both by nature and by experience. The composer's *scientia bene modulandi* must be taken seriously as a science, self-consciously applied to producing 'musical feeling' in the listener. The psychology of music is a proper part of the composer's art, and Hindemith has no patience with the romantic contrast between art and science; for this contrast depended upon regarding the composer's work as a form of self-expression, or of expression of feeling; and this is a mere metaphor, which Hindemith easily derides. In considering the emotional effects of music. Hindemith again, and characteristically, takes the standpoint of the listener, upon whom the composer must operate scientifically. It is a fact that music, intelligently heard, produces 'emotional reactions', and the composer must understand the psychology of musical feeling if he is to contrive his proper effects. Hindemith therefore has a psychological explanation of 'perceiving music emotionally' to match his psychological theory of 'perceiving music intellectually'; and this explanation also has no experimental evidence to support it. He plausibly argues that the phrase 'the language of music' is a misleading metaphor which conceals rather than solves the problem; and, secondly, that the emotional suggestiveness of music is not derived from its direct or indirect representation of actual sound. There must be some psychological link between particular musical structures and the emotions which they evoke. His own theory is that emotional reactions to music are the images or memories of original feelings, not original feelings themselves; and he takes this identification to be a matter of fact, since he deduces from it the conclusion that '"musical" gaiety can be felt only if a feeling of real gaiety is already known to us' (p. 39). 'If, for example, we assume that music is able to arouse a reaction, which in the mind of a mass murderer uncovers the memory of the satisfaction he felt after having slaughtered a row of twenty victims, that feeling cannot be reproduced in our own minds unless we do as he did – murder twenty people and then listen to the adequate music.'

Here is total confusion, and the confusion must be

traced back to its source. To regard music, or any of the
arts, as means of reproducing in less vivid form feelings
already experienced is certainly not to take the art seriously; and it is a primitive psychology which supposes
that all feeling must originally arise from 'experience'.
Why should not the 'musical impression' bring its own
satisfaction, its own musical gaiety, musical sadness, sense
of cruelty even, with it? Why should it be assumed that
'experience' excludes musical experience, and that only
events in a man's biography can originally evoke his
feelings? The answer to these rhetorical questions is—
metaphysical prejudice; for our only evidence of fact is
that certain musical structures evoke immense satisfaction,
and in addition seem in themselves gay or sad or harsh
or noble or restless. When these epithets are applied, in
an effort to convey something of a musical impression in
non-musical terms, no statement is being made about the
listener's emotions. It is the music that is gay, and not
the listener. Sad music is not music that makes the
listener (palely) sad; it may produce, and often does
produce, a great elation. These terms—'sad', 'gay', 'harsh'
—are applied to music by analogy, and not to describe a
literal effect—as if music were being used as a powerful
psychological medicine. Music, and works of art in
general, are not seriously to be regarded as substitutes for
first-hand experience, designed to produce images or
memories of common human feeling; they bring their
own moods and feelings with them. One may speak of
colours, or of any arrangement of colours, as harsh or
violent, without implying that they induce a mood of
harshness or violence in the spectator. The epithets
describe the visual impression and not the psychological

effect. And so epithets of feeling applied to works of music describe the musical feeling or impression, and not the remote reactions of the particular listeners.

The fatal transition in Hindemith's argument occurs early in the book, on page 35: he writes: 'The term "musical feeling" is vague and ambiguous: it may have completely different meanings to different persons. If we replace it with "emotional reactions", we know more precisely what is meant . . . musical structures impress us. . . . We are touched emotionally. Some structures are sad, sound sad, express sadness, or make us sad–or whatever commonplace expressions may be used to describe this fact.' Every important difference is blurred in this passage. There is, first, the intense satisfaction or pleasure that the music itself may give, when it 'impresses us in a purely musical fashion' (p. 32): and this purely musical satisfaction or pleasure is itself an emotion or feeling. Secondly, there is the mood or 'feeling' (in another sense) of the music, which immediately suggests, or is associated with, certain emotions which we have experienced. Because the music, for natural or historical reasons, is associated in our minds with these emotions, we recall or think or these emotions when we hear it, and this involuntary memory may bring very great pleasure, and also an emotion of its own. Thirdly, the listener follows the style, or the steps, in the musical thought of the composer, and is acquainted with the mind and musical feeling of the composer, as one may recognize and enjoy a painter's feeling for form and colour. Here the word 'feeling' has again changed its sense. The deliberate, informed art (*scientia*) of the composer is spent on the musical structure itself and on producing the purely musical impression.

Perhaps he may also set himself to play upon the manifold external associations in the minds of his audience, and even, at the risk of mannerism, self-consciously emphasize his own characteristic habits of musical thought. But such planning must surely be so utterly different in kind as scarcely to deserve the name of *scientia*, which Hindemith gives to it; and such remote effects are neither necessary nor sufficient conditions of the first, purely musical (or aesthetic) satisfaction (p. 28), which a work of music must give. The full enjoyment of the music constitutes in itself a feeling or emotion, and there is no need to look further to 'explain' this fact. That people are musical is a fact about them which is as primitive as the fact that they like to dance. Scientists may be left to find the causes and conditions of being musical or of liking to dance. But there is no need to derive musical feeling from the personal feelings of active life.

From the beginning of the book there is the constant assumption that music is not taken seriously unless it is shown to have some effect on ordinary practical life; so there are references to 'the ethical power of music' and the 'moral strength' that it must give. This equation – if serious, then moral – is the equation of puritanism, as if the achievements of art had always to be justified as means to something more solid than themselves. They may sometimes give 'moral strength', but to regard works of art as psychological medicine is scarcely to take them seriously. Rather one might argue that the fact that men are capable of such achievements is a source of 'moral strength' to anyone who attends to the history of art. The 'seriousness' does not reside in the psychological effects of the particular works, but in the fact of human achievement.

To the musical person, music is as much a world of experience, directly involving his thoughts and feelings, as are his personal relations or any of his activities. He is as much a listening being as he is a practically active one; and he does not need to satisfy himself that his listening has some good effect on his practical activities. The composer, on his side, is free to create whatever seems to him to add to the range of this experience, and he will betray his own musical thought and feeling in his style. No one can anticipate the limits of achievement in music or what work may be done in the future: least of all on the basis of *a priori* psychology. One can only examine experiments in form and technique already made and mark where they have so far failed; and this is part of the subject of the later, less philosophical chapters of this interesting book, which is so sternly conservative and Lutheran in its attitudes; for it is assumed that the composer has some duty to the listener or some responsibility for the effects of his work upon the public. But if he has brought into existence a musical structure, which has its own qualities of musical thought and musical feeling, that is surely the whole of his duty, even if no one understands him for a thousand years, and even if human life disappears. The music is there and so (for morality) is the achievement. A work of music is not great and noble because of the greatness and nobility which it may engender. These are no less intrinsic qualities of musical structures, as we perceive them, than of practical policies, as we perceive them; and the emotion associated with the perception of these qualities may be equally direct and original in both cases. That art must somehow be an imitation of reality is a Platonic prejudice, and this prejudice reappears in the doctrine that the emotions that art arouses must be shadows of real emotions. But a musical structure is no less real than St. Paul's, and my experience of it no less a real experience, which equally calls into play thought and feeling; and I may receive impressions of gaiety and nobility from the one as from the other. The composer can be responsible only for the vividness of the musical impression, and not for the listener's further reactions. He may plan to make the music gay, but he wastes his talent if he plans to make me gay. His whole work is done, and the rest of the world is well-served, if he has added a new, musically solid, object to the sum of possible experience, and if his work has a character of its own, and if, whatever its various psychological effects, it makes its own impression of achievement.

But these last statements of mine are matters of opinion only, and largely of moral opinion.

21

Modern Tragedy

Raymond Williams' *Modern Tragedy*[1] is 'about the connections, in modern tragedy, between event and experience and idea, and its form is designed at once to explore and to emphasise these radical connections'. Mr. Williams employs an imaginative sociology of his own. With its aid he sees in contemporary literature a true reflection of the dislocation of private lives, which, he believes, no longer keep a natural connection with a continuing social life in a community, accepted and enjoyed. His vision is of a possible lost Eden, of a wholeness falling away into fragments; the metaphor of a torn social fabric is essential to the vision. One must suspect that this particular diagnosis of the disease of modernity is itself part of the condition diagnosed. This kind of imaginative sociology, in the tradition of Carlyle and Ruskin, may itself be an expression of a modern literary temperament, and a convenient myth for intellectuals who are uneasy in an industrial environment.

One finds oneself wandering around in a circle, from the imagined social experience to the dramatic literature, and from the literature to the social experience; there is a pattern of interpretation, but no independent confirmation that anything is explained by the pattern. Lukacs' famous studies of Scott and Balzac have opened the way for this strangely intuitive, yet historical, criticism of literature.

[1] Chatto & Windus, 1966.

It amounts to a reversal of Marxism, for a supposed social consciousness replaces any hard, materialistic analysis of social facts as a basis for understanding the decay of literary forms. One may perhaps convince oneself, one may have a dim feeling, that this fragmentation of the social fabric, first suggested by Schiller and Hegel, is a real feature of modern experience, separately identifiable, and not just a familiar theme, and a recurring fiction, of the imagination. But literary criticism in this style will still seem a prosaic substitute for the original writing that it interprets. Criticism becomes a programme for, or a preface to, a possible fiction, and approaches the condition of fiction itself.

The historical-imaginative style of criticism has become so familiar, as a separate literary genre, that one overlooks the enormity of the assumptions that must be made if it is to be taken literally. Are we to suppose that men's dreams change with changing social relations? Is there not an imagery, and are there not associated themes of fantasy and fiction, which are independent of any adult consciousness of learnt social relations? It has been plausibly suggested that the sources of the interest we take in tragic action on the stage are not unrelated to the religious feelings that surround the doctrines of the Fall, of Judgment, of predestination and salvation. The doctrinal setting of these inchoate ideas may change from period to period; the social setting in which they present themselves will certainly change. The shape and sonority of sentences, the quality of the rhetoric, will change correspondingly. These are changes that touch the surface of the mind, and are a proper part of the history of drama as a history of styles. They may even help to explain its abrupt decays and rebirths. But surely the substance of an interest in tragedy cannot be found here; for the sources of the philosophical ideas that make an action, represented or real, a tragic action are primarily the subject-matter of individual psychology, if not of philosophy.

A tragic disappointment is one that admits of no remedy in social action, or in any alteration of the specific conditions of the action. The disappointment lies in the nature of the action itself, as intrinsically liable to accident and mistake, and also in the double face of virtue as carrying its own defect with it, a returning echo that mocks the agent's first intention. Enjoyment of tragedy marks a point of breakdown in the hold that moral ideas have upon us, a breakdown that is the more strongly felt in proportion as moral ideas are clearly defined. This is one place of entry for tragedy, familiar to everyone from their intimate experience. Morality presupposes a relation that is humanly intelligible between intention and achievement, and it has usually presupposed also an inhuman, natural or real, justice upon which human justice can be built. But even in childhood, the relation between intention and achievement is felt to be insecure. Filial and other loyalties are too often combined with thoughts of murder and treason, and the clear-sighted repair of wrong in the house too often turns out to be its destruction. So the judgment of action is shifted towards its consequences, where one knows that, from the standpoint of morality, it should not be.

It is not so much that a great ambition, the will to positive action and to repair the disjointed world, fails catastrophically in a tragic situation. Rather the action fails in a particular way and for a particular reason; the forces used are not, as they seem to be, the forces that really control human fortunes. These are always in tragedy invisible to the protagonist until it is too late, and are therefore unusable, and appear, to us and to him, as accidents. So the distinction between willed or voluntary evil and involuntary evil is made to seem tenuous and uncertain, a human pretence; and yet any justifiable moral attitude requires the distinction. One may come to think that what one has achieved, not intentionally but seemingly by accident, is more indicative of one's true nature than the original intentions were.

One may be born to become blind, and at the centre of conflicting forces which remain unrecognized until it is too late; and precisely this blindness may be the condition of resolute action and high intentions. Anna Karenina takes action to escape from a dead life, and finally kills herself, because of the accident, as it seems, of Vronsky's carelessness, restlessness and casual absence. The story becomes a tragedy, because of the uncharted necessities of natural law which are revealed in the lives surrounding hers. The justifiable action that should save her, and repair a loss, becomes a waste and destruction of her life, just because it was too strongly willed, or willed with a single mind, blindly. For the tragic consciousness, a strong will to put things right will end in mistake and self-destruction, because the sources of wrong are too remote, and beyond the reach of any solitary virtue. The sources of evil are in the house and in the family. Once disjointed, house and family are locked together in a natural misfortune, which no individual energy can suddenly break.

Ibsen provides the obvious examples of modern tragedy: modern, just because virtue takes the form in his plays of action against a social wrong, or at least against an offence to conscience or to bourgeois freedom. The pride of improvement and liberation ends in waste and destruction, leaving the survivors with their inherited stain, as if it were the shared wrong which had held them together. Within the play there has been single-minded action, and not pathos; but the liberal intentions have been shown to depend upon an ignorance, or an ignoring, of the genealogy of misfortunes, which pass across the generations as an inherited punishment. The family, as Ibsen classically represented it, is not merely a social unit. Its links are more constant and less open to inspection, and, above all, less voluntary and less adjustable at will. Unhappy families are, as Tolstoy wrote, different from each other, fiercely coherent in their attachment to a distinguishing doom. Liberalism and the modern spirit, as Ibsen knew them, try to dismiss tragic inheritances, on the assumption that the quality of an individual life may always be rationally changed in a single generation. Ibsen was on both sides, seeing at once the modern necessity to believe in enlightenment and in the power of the individual to escape from his inheritance, and the old desperate implausibility of this reformer's assumption.

It is at least possible that the criticism that sees literature, unquestioningly, as criticism of society is itself a symptom of the decline which the critics think that they notice. The philosophical idea of tragedy requires a kind of confident individualism which no historically-minded critic will retain. The necessary isolation of the individual, alone with his intention and its consequences, will seem untruthful to the historian, unless some trailing edges of social analysis are added. But in the setting of tragedy the social pressures on the individual are uninteresting, because they explain too much, and by the wrong kind of causality. As sometimes in Brecht, the protagonists become pathetic, victims of their historical circumstances, figures in a pageant.

There is a striking consensus in writings about tragedy, which cuts across differences of time and place. It would indeed be strange if the nature of the interest in tragedy changed with changing social conditions, at least within societies which recognize a rational morality, whether secular or religious. The contrast between tragic consequences, and the catastrophes that follow imputable errors, cannot be ignored, as long as justice and rational reward and punishment are taken seriously. Is a man responsible for the destructive consequences, when he finds that, with the best of intentions, he has only acted out, and brought to a conclusion, the old family conflicts? The excitement of a tragic action on the stage is in part the reflection of the dizziness, or loss of balance, that is left in one's mind by a representation of the absurdly narrow limits of free-will.

22

A Ruinous Conflict

For at least a century and a half there has been a continuing argument in European literature about the
aesthetic education of men who must live in industrial
societies. There have been great edifices of theory, as in
Schiller and Marx; or more or less inspired reflection, as in
Blake, Carlyle, Arnold, Flaubert, Ruskin, Morris, Eliot,
Tawney, F. R. Leavis, and many others. The problem is
obviously a real one, and it need not be stated too impre-
cisely. The accelerating production of wealth entails
constantly increasing division of labour; accelerating
scientific discovery entails constantly increasing specialization of knowledge and of work. Is it possible, and is it
desirable, to arrest these processes? If not, how can the
consequent impairments of individual intelligence and
sensibility be made good?

Drawing the terms of his philosophy of art from Kant's
Critique of Judgment, Schiller attempted a systematic defence
of poetry, and an apology for aesthetic experience, in his
Letters on the Aesthetic Education of Man. In the sixth letter
he wrote:

With us moderns the image of the race is scattered
. . . in a fragmentary way, so that you have to go the
rounds from individual to individual in order to gather
the totality of the race. With us, one may be inclined
to assert, the mental faculties show themselves de-

tached in operation, as psychology separates them in idea, and we see not merely individual persons, but whole classes of human beings, developing only a part of their capacities, while the rest of them, like a stunted plant, show only a feeble vestige of their nature. . . . It was culture itself that inflicted this wound upon modern humanity. As soon as enlarged experience and more precise speculation made necessary a sharper division of the sciences on the one hand, and, on the other, the more intricate machinery of states made necessary a more rigorous dissociation of ranks and occupations, the essential bond of human nature was torn about, and a ruinous conflict set its harmonious powers at variance. . . . Man [now] never develops the harmony of his being, and instead of imprinting humanity upon his nature, he becomes merely the imprint of his occupation, of his science. . . . And so gradually individual concrete life is extinguished, in order that the abstract life of the whole may prolong its sorry existence.

Schiller did not confine himself to denunciation:

Partiality in the exercise of powers, it is true, inevitably leads the individual into error, but the race to truth.

This sets the problem. Is there a solution in education?

We may decide to mean by 'culture' all that is included under education, without thinking of education as confined to youth. At most ages we continue to acquire knowledge and to learn to understand and to enjoy what was previously unintelligible to us. Some of this knowledge and understanding may be exercised freely and without regard to its uses: in play, in sport, and in the arts, but also in scientific curiosity, when this is an immediate source of satisfaction. It is certain that what we learn and enjoy, and therefore our culture, will still be determined, at least in part, by the particular skills required in the present phase of social organization. But there is a margin of freedom within which we can deliberate about and plan for culture: first, because we can change some features of the organization of work by political action; secondly, because with increasing wealth there is an increasing sphere of freedom beyond the necessities of work. In their two lectures[1] neither Sir Charles Snow nor Dr. Leavis deliberated at length about the first alternative: culture under socialism, culture under capitalism, was not the issue. Indeed, in his strictures on British culture as it is, Dr. Leavis ignored the economic and political determinants of it. For I do not believe that, in standing up for the Bushmen, he was recommending that we should organize our work as they do (or did). To concentrate in this way on the superstructure, on the nature of literacy and intelligence in the abstract, is to rob the difficult discussion of many of its difficulties.

Most of us cannot wander from country to country, like Lawrence, or discover our own conditions for creative work; nor will this seem a possible plan of education for our descendants. The advantages of literacy, and the proper interpretation of it, have to be related to our social circumstances. Dr. Leavis's own critical thought has

[1] 'The Two Cultures and the Scientific Revolution', 1959 (C. P. Snow), and 'Two Cultures? The Significance of C. P. Snow' 1962 (F. R. Leavis).

in fact been brought into relation with political action through its influence on the New Left in Britain and on educational theorists. Therefore we may concentrate on Britain and America as they now are, and as they might be, and be less concerned with the full life, and the quick perceptions, that we might enjoy as resident tourists in Taos.

There are some false oppositions that must first be cleared away. Reason and imagination take many forms and it is an error to identify them, as powers of mind, with one of their specific forms of expression. The same powers of mind which, in the seventeenth century, might simultaneously be expressed in the study of optics and in the construction of a metaphysical system, might now be expressed in a discipline that has another title (perhaps in mathematical logic or theoretical physics or statistical theory). More generally, science, interpreted as the systematic study of the natural order, has absorbed a large part of what was previously called philosophy, and mathematics has absorbed another fraction of this original whole. The propensity to speculate, and to look for exact and general solutions to the most abstract questions, is no longer peculiarly, or even mainly, the mark of philosophers. They are the residuary legatees of a great estate now divided into many allotments. The study of literature and the study of history have also changed their scope, though less dramatically and abruptly. Modern scholarship sometimes aims at the exactness of the sciences; and the social sciences now intrude upon some domains of literary speculation. The problem of education and contemporary culture is therefore mis-stated as some kind of inter-disciplinary struggle, as a need for a treaty, or non-aggression pact, between the disciplines.

The disciplines change their titles and their territories; the balance that has to be found is rather between common powers of mind that are independently identifiable. Secondly, it is mere snobbery to segregate science from the humanities with the claim that scientists are concerned with the quantitative aspects of reality, and the humanities with qualitative distinctions, as if scientists were 'in trade', while those who study history and the arts were the true gentlemen of the intellect, cultivating their inherited land. Bergson, and many other Canutes who have wanted to set a limit to scientific advance, have invoked this doubtful distinction. It is not clear, and it presupposes a crude account of the sciences.

It is at least clear, first, that men learn to use their intellect and their senses to explore reality, and, secondly, that they have impulses and emotions that become attached to persons and objects in the external world. In their development towards maturity both these aspects of their mind must be trained together, and either, or both, may be stunted or distorted. In exploring reality they learn to distinguish fact from fiction, the complex reality from their over-simplifying demands and wishes. They learn to be objective, to allow their expectations to be rebuffed by external objects that will not fit their designs. In this education they learn that they are confined in a small place within a world of objects that stretches far beyond the limits of their knowledge and control. They learn that they can at best only be contributors to knowledge within a long co-operative inquiry that presses the division of labour to its extreme point.

But they do not, and cannot, become cognitive machines. Their impulses and emotions are also being trained, and find their forms of expression in various fictions, in free experiments in styles of speech and behaviour. Submission to external reality, respect for disappointing fact, calls for compensations: in illusion, in the willing suspense of logic and of argument, in the intelligent rearrangement of the external world to reflect private and personal expectations. It is a condition of sanity that a point of balance between wish and reality, between ordered illusion and ordered fact, should be found and preserved without confusion between them, and without the mind being split into two halves. One can now easily imagine a society of the future in which rational men, scientists, technicians, and administrators, divide their public from their private interests, their skills from their entertainment, and, drugged by communal amusements, confine intelligence to its purely cognitive and practical uses. They would be emotionally and sensuously undeveloped, interested only in common methods tested by results, and indifferent to personal styles in expression and communication. They would be split, strained, and distorted to the point of insanity. Alternatively, one can read or hear–there is no need to imagine them–the opinions and attitudes of those who must have large views of the world which are their private property, and who cannot bear to look at the refractory public facts. Maturity, as an aim of education, demands an integral intelligence, which is at ease both with factual investigations of reality and also with wild, but ordered and significant, reconstructions of it.

If we are to consider the claims of a literary education, it is relevant to notice that many, perhaps most, of the most influential writers of this century–Conrad, Yeats,

Eliot, Lawrence, among others–have for their different reasons tried to belittle the contemporary scientific culture, together with the tradition of rational inquiry on which it was based; and they have deplored its social and political consequences. It has been common ground among them that welfare and diffused opportunity have not led to an enriched imaginative experience, and that a more noble, integrated society was lost somewhere in the past. The greatest writers of this time have generally been critics of democracy and progress from some aristocratic point of view. But this dissociation of the writer, this negative, destructive element, is not to be counted against an aesthetic, or literary, education. On the contrary, it is the strength and purpose of an aesthetic education, and of the study of literature and of the visual arts, that they counter-balance and lighten the increasing burden of social utility and of social order.

When a writer is felt to be, in this sense, subversive and disaffected, he restores, in some vivid form, the memory of a private, unconsenting self, a lost rebellion; he may often be felt to be recapturing inner experience, to be representing a reality which cannot be otherwise acknow-ledged, or even seen. We have less and less need of poetry, fiction, and the visual arts for the exploration of social realities, as we have more and more need of them for questioning the advertised claims of these realities upon us, and for indirectly revealing disavowed forms of experi-ence that are in conflict with social roles. Educated in the physical and social sciences, competent in logic, the virtu-ous citizen with an understanding of 'the modern world' can still be lost, and know that the greater part of his experience and his feeling is inaccessible to his intelligence, unrealized and uninterpreted. He can be dazed and deadened by abstractions, as Schiller foresaw, and by the strain of concentrating his interests, and of narrowing his faculties, for the presumed benefit of a general progress. We turn to imaginative literature, and to the visual arts, as to an ordered carnival in which, with customary identities masked and reversed, a common humanity is restored in a new order and enjoyed without restrictions. The mask of fiction, or of illusion, is not a form of escape or concealment; for the 'true' identity always remains, as a consequence of its many reversals in art, questionable and ambiguous. We can no longer take a social require-ment as Nature, or be sure that there is such a thing as a natural self, closed and coherent.

It is a depressing error of social realists, to suppose that 'important' themes (for example, 'the Corridors of Power') are important, and that an art naïvely relevant to 'con-temporary realities' is the relevant art of the time. We look to literature and the visual arts for significant re-definitions of reality beyond the categories of journalism, 'significant' as pointing to unnoticed experience, and as suggesting possibilities within us which have been excluded by social arrangements. We commonly find these re-definitions in original poems, fiction, and painting, which disturb the sense of an imposed social congruence, and which are animated by a hatred, expressed or unexpressed, of the losses in individual energy that are entailed.

There is therefore a special case for some education in the humanities being an ingredient in the education of everyone. There are two related reasons for this: first, that it is a condition of sanity that the unsocialized levels of the mind should be given some ordered, concrete embodiment, and thereby made accessible to intelligence and enjoyment; secondly, that through works of art we communicate in a common enjoyment, and a common understanding, across the barriers of specialized interests. Each man his own critic of the arts is therefore a clear ideal of education.

Each man his own compendium of the sciences is not. The second law of thermodynamics is only significant in its setting and as part of a physical theory. By itself, it is almost as inert and unengaging as the date of the battle of Hastings. A human faculty is plainly stunted if a man has not learnt what objectivity is in some scientific discipline that requires conclusiveness, absolute accuracy in result, and that is free from the ambiguity and uncertainty of any aesthetic inquiry. But this does not demand, as a necessary ingredient in education, that we should share a common range of allusion to scientific results. In this sphere, unlike the arts, communication passes through shared methods rather than through results. Numeracy does not essentially consist in a range of allusion, or even in being familiar with particular landmarks of science. It is rather the equipment that enables one to enter the territory of natural science at any point that one chooses and, once inside, to follow a path of argument. As it is a human (not social) loss not to have read a part of the literature of our own language, so it is a human loss, a kind of lameness, to be unable to follow mathematical and inductive reasoning.

The problem of a full education is primarily a political and economic one, and must be solved mainly by political action, as is now beginning to be recognized. The opportunity of full literacy and numeracy is no longer the unchallenged privilege of a ruling class, together with a few exceptionally able recruits to this class, as it used to be; nor is the opportunity open and equal, as a recognized right, as it might be in a socialist state. We are in a half-way position, as we once were in respect of public health. During this interval the more controversy, and the more publicity, for any of the issues, the better. A volley of abuse in Cambridge, an angry outburst anywhere, may still lead, however indirectly and unpleasantly, towards an effective demand for political action. Students will not, in the long run, acquiesce in a too stringent, and too early, adaptation to a social rôle. They will naturally look for more eloquence, more variety in learning, a temporary disorder and a moratorium on progress, as a condition of sanity.

Index

INDEX

INDEX

A Note About the Author

Stuart N. Hampshire

was born in Lincolnshire, England, in 1914 and was educated at Repton and Balliol College, Oxford. Professor Hampshire has been Lecturer in Philosophy, University College, London; Fellow of New College, Oxford; Research Fellow, All Souls College; Grote Professor of Philosophy of Mind and Logic, University College, London. Since 1963 Professor Hampshire has been Professor and Chairman of the Department of Philosophy at Princeton University.

ABIGAIL E. WEEKS MEMORIAL LIBRARY
UNION COLLEGE
BARBOURVILLE, KENTUCKY

809
H231

Hampshire

Modern writers and other essays